ACCLAIM FOR MY OWN WAY OF BEING

Vida is a force of nature. Highly recommended for anyone seeking wisdom and inspiration.

DOMINIQUE LAMY, ACTRESS, AUTHOR OF HOW TO IGNITE YOUR INNER STRENGTH TO EXPAND AND MANIFEST YOUR PERSONAL ESSENCE

Vida is an artist with words, creating word pictures in both her prose and poetry. You will find many nuggets of wisdom in this book, her gift of self to the world. Thank you, Vida.

DINAH LIN, MBA, INSPIRATIONAL SPEAKER AND BEST-SELLING AUTHOR OF DARING TO DREAM ONCE AGAIN – IT'S NEVER TOO LATE!

My Own Way of Being begins with generational trauma and ultimately reveals the miraculous impact of intentional self-awareness. Vida's journey of growth is an inspiration. I love this woman!

LONNIE WEISS, ORGANIZATIONAL CONSULTANT, MEETING DESIGNER AND FACILITATOR AND LONG-STANDING FRIEND

Wow! What an inspiration! Vida shows us that only by facing the reality of your family can you we it to create a path for ourselves – one that ends in a life well lived.

JAN FRIEDMAN, MSW AND LONG-STANDING FRIEND

Vida's memoir is gripping and powerful, demonstrating how pain and challenges can be transformed into gifts through the curiosity and inquiry of an open heart.

AUDREY SEYMOUR, FOUNDER, C

D1607768

In *My Own Way of Being* Vida Groman shares her magical gift of summoning divinely perfect words to capture the sacredness of life, as she calls it, in all its heart-rending and precious essence – joy and growth, death and loss, discovery and rebirth. Highly recommended. This book will touch your soul.

JULIE ANN TURNER, BEST-SELLING AUTHOR OF GENESIS OF GENIUS & HOST, GLOBAL CONSCIOUSSHIFT SHOW RENAISSANCEGENIUS.COM

Vida Groman creates magic with her language, blending her memoir with powerful insights and deep wisdom, and in the same breath, inviting us to reflect deeply on our own life. All is expressed in poetic prose that is asking of us, too, to have the courage to "live fully alive."

AMARA HAMILTON, LIFE COACH, TEACHER AND ENERGY CLEARING EXPERT

Vida uses the metaphor of a tree to describe her own growth through adversity, hardship and struggle into someone powerful, brave and wise.

DAPHNE COHN, WRITER, INTUITIVE DANCER, PRIESTESS

Coupled with beautiful imagery of natural growth, this sparkling memoir provides an easy-to-follow pathway through Vida's life so far, inviting us to deeply reflect on our own.

ANNIE POWELL, AUTHOR, FACILITATOR, LIVING FROM YOUR LIGHT

VIDA GROMAN

MY OWN WAY OF BEING

THE COURAGE TO BE DIFFERENT

Published by Deep Pacific Press

117 E 37th St. #580, Loveland, Colorado 80538

Deep
Pacific
Press

DeepPacificPress.com

email: support@vidagroman.com

www.vidagroman.com

ISBN 978-1-956108-28-6 (paperback)
ISBN 978-1-956108-29-3 (eBook)

Cover design & illustration: Patrick Knowles

Interior illustrations: Christine Banman

Interior design & formatting: Mark Thomas / Coverness.com

Dedication

To my mother, Ruth Shapiro Groman.

To my father, Jacob Groman.

To my sister, Michele Groman Millinger.

Without you, where would I be today?

*You are the soil I grew up in and you
have helped make me
who I am.*

Deepest gratitude.

My Own Way Of Being

The High View

To see the big picture...
the pieces that make up the journey

What a good way to begin.

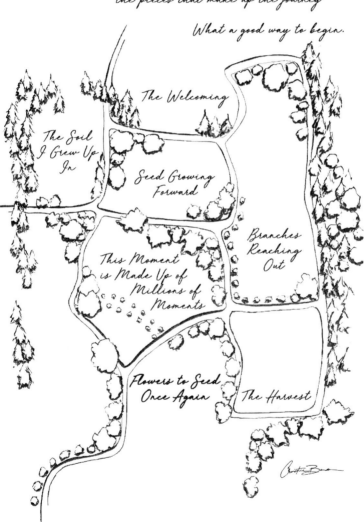

The Welcoming

The Soil
I Grew Up
In

Seed Growing
Forward

Branches
Reaching
Out

This Moment
is Made Up of
Millions of
Moments

Flowers to Seed
Once Again

The Harvest

The High View

This moment is made up of the millions of moments that got me to this point. In total, seventy-three years' worth of moments. While meditating several years ago, I was told to write a book about my life, that I had lived long enough to have stories to tell and wisdom to share, and that it was time to take a close look at "who I am."

You can be in the middle of the journey without ever stepping back to reflect on where you have come from, where you currently are, and where you want to go. This is the time for my reflection.

I welcome you to journey with me as I share my story of living a *beloved life* through the travails of trauma and sorrows. I believe Life is Sacred, and it is worth living. You might say I had no choice other than to believe Life is Sacred; after all, I was named Vida, which means Beloved Life.

Within that Beloved Life, sometimes we are given hardships, difficult childhoods, and loneliness. At first, amid those experiences, we believe it is all bad. But at some point, if we allow ourselves to, we just might find the gifts we gathered to live through to the other side.

Here is the High View of this book...

The Soil I Grew Up In

I come from generations of hardship, terror, and poverty. I also come from educated, intuitive, creative people. All this lives in me. I have inherited these experiences and the qualities and strengths that resulted in my family surviving and thriving.

I am a child of that history.

There were many players. Let's start with my father, Jack, who had to cut down his father, Isadore. Unable to make a living for his family during the depression, Isadore decided to hang himself in the entrance way to the family's apartment. Lena, Jack's mother (my grandmother,) then had to raise two boys alone in poverty and decided to harden her heart against the world.

My mother, Ruth, escaped with her family from Poland when she was four years old, right before a Pogrom ravaged their village (pogrom is a Russian word used to describe violent destruction, generally of a Jewish population.) Hers was a story about the strength of immigrants leaving their homeland to create safety and a new life in a strange country.

My great aunt, Tonta Frumi, acted like a grandmother to me. Her tender love and acceptance of me provided ground for me to stand on. Then there's my cousin, Adolph, my ally and support as I stepped into my truth around my sexuality.

I was given just the perfect set of players to teach me about resilience, creativity, and yearning for something more.

That was the soil I grew up in.

Seed Growing Forward

I grew up with adversity. And I grew up with emotional and physical abuse. I found allies. My mother knew I was a sensitive and empathic child, and she did what she could. An unexpected ally was my cat: Fluffy saved my life so many times as she mothered me with her attention and love. Unconditional love, she expected nothing from me but touch.

Growing up was also a time for making decisions about my personality and how I would live life. Some of my decisions and beliefs had far-reaching negative effects. My ability to use my voice, to speak up, became stunted when I was five. It seems I said something that deeply upset my cousin. My aunt, her mother, convinced me I was a horrible person for using words to hurt others. One event can affect the rest of your life, and this one did, affecting when I spoke, how I spoke, or if I spoke up. It left me muted for a long time.

I grew without much guidance from my parents, who both lived with fear. I suppose that might have been a blessing, as their lack of guidance left me having to figure things out. I learned not to depend on others or even to ask for help. In my current life, I am still working on asking for and receiving help from others.

Intensity was my friend. I lived in a young body filled with deep emotions and sensations and no real way to express any of that in words, which left me feeling isolated and lonely.

Nothing that I experienced in my early years was in vain. A hunger and yearning grew in me to find other ways of being. I hungered to find people who would "get me." That hunger moved me forward.

Branches Reaching Out

It was time to take myself seriously, to find the courage to be me as fully as I could be. Being "me" meant I had to claim and embrace my sexuality and my spirituality. Coming out to those two truths opened me up and I learned how to be with myself comfortably, peacefully.

I learned how to be open to attracting and loving a woman, one woman, for over twenty-five years.

I learned how to let go, too. In that time of my life when I was stepping onto my true path, I had to face losing my mother, and later, my partner. Death taught me much as life became even more sacred.

Those years were the "stretching-out" years, yet conversely, the "reaching inward and finding me" years.

Flower to Seed Once Again

My flowering years were filled with learning and teaching. I was blessed to find wonderful teachers who taught me skills and tools about living authentically. They taught by example, sharing knowledge they had gained through the living of their lives.

Dawna Markova helped me uncover how I received and how I expressed myself in the world. Without her teachings, I would never understand how to find my words.

Alice Tredway introduced me to lives past and present. She lovingly opened me up to other possible levels of life, and she treated me with such respect.

Mary Ebert was my writing angel. Without her encouragement, I am not sure I would have written a word.

I soaked up every morsel these incredible women gave me so I could turn around and offer my knowledge to other women. My work was being born during that time, born and refined.

This Moment is Made of a Million Other Moments

At last, I find myself here and now. I am looking backward and forward to see what I have learned, and what I still want to offer. This moment is the reflection on my life.

I offer my blessing that I wrote to myself many years ago:

I still desire the connection to life. I feel
blessed to have been given all that was
mine and I am grateful I chose to use what
was mine to heal and grow, and most
importantly, to support other women in
their journey.

May my journey continue.

The Harvest

I ask what this book wants me to know, and what lessons it wants to teach me. I believe this book has its own energy and life force.

There are three lessons that I share here:

The importance of facing where we have come from, the power of honoring who we really are, and the gift of the mentors and teachers all around us.

I open my hands... to you
I open my heart... to you

Welcome to my Journey.

The Welcoming

I dedicate this book to you, the reader,
and your journey back to yourself.

For all the trips that got cancelled in my
life, I also dedicate this book to the one
trip, the one journey that did occur and
is still occurring – the journey of my
life.

May you say "yes" to your life's journey.
It is absolutely worth the trip home to
yourself.

The Invitation

I am not a religious person, nor someone who follows a traditional path.

I am, however, deeply connected to Spirit, my Divine Partner.

I connect in my own way. When I asked for guidance about writing this book, I was told to be honest, totally honest, and to talk to you, the reader, as if we were sitting together having a cup of something, hanging out, and talking about life. That is what I have done with every page, with a cup of something in my hand, imagining you sitting here with me. Those mental images are some of my favorite moments.

With joy in my heart, I offer my life as an example of how to come from darkness, own that darkness, want more, find more, and come out the other side into the light. If I can do it, and I am still doing it, so can you. I once told one of my teachers I must be the slowest learner on earth – I started at age ten and am now seventy-three, and still learning.

I offer this book as an invitation to step into your humanity – all of it – the good, the bad, and even the ugly.

We are all vulnerable to our own cracks,
our own wounds and hurts.

We are also all able to shine our light,
do good, love and be loved, for we are
made of sparks of the Divine.

We are human in our receiving and divine in our giving. This is the time we live in on the planet. When the pandemic began, I decided to ask the virus what it wanted us to know. This is what I heard, "We are demanding that you remember who and what you really are. You have gotten so far away from remembering your truth of being. You are all one. Remember it."

Through my stories and ponderings, I hope to open your memories of being human so you might wrap your own arms around you, pull yourself gently to your own breast, say words of comfort for your ears to hear, then sit down and have a cup of something.

I have asked myself a million times why I wanted to write this book, and equally, who would want to read these stories and reflections from my life. I suppose those are common questions for most when they begin to write a book. I could have spent a lot of time trying to find the answers to those two questions, but what a waste of energy that would have been. And to quote from Charles Mackesy's book, *The Boy, The Mole, The Fox and The Horse,* when the little boy asked the mole:

> *"What do you think is the biggest waste*
> *of time?"*

> *"Comparing yourself to others,"*
> *said the mole.*

So, it really doesn't matter who might want to read this book, or not. It may not even matter why I wrote this book. I just knew I had to. For me. You just happened to pick it up for some reason. Something drew you to open this book. I may wonder what it is, but only you know. Trust that. Let yourself follow that and be open to receive what is yours to receive. I don't believe there are any accidents.

No matter how you found your way here…

I WELCOME YOU!!!

This book is about life, my life for sure, but life in general, and how sacred it is to be alive. I'd love to share the words that came through me about the sacredness of life with you.

The Sacredness of Life

The first seed was planted by the invisible hands
of the universe,
Into the earth of dirt, soil, minerals,
It sat in darkness, in stillness.
No thinking, no planning,
Sitting in silence,
Allowing itself to be.

And then from inside, a stirring emerged,
Vibrations quaking till the shell of enclosure
broke open.
The innate knowing of every element inside
knew,
as if by magic,
To reach up, and up, toward something.

It was the light.
The knowing was reaching for the light.
That knowing followed an unseen urge,
Up, and up, and up, till…

It broke the surface and rose above the darkness,
Light shone down, warming every element and
cell.
With that encouraging warmth, the seed became
a stalk.
That stalk grew into a trunk and became stronger
and thicker, had substance,
Strength to stand tall.

And it grew strong and up,
Growing branches wide and high.
And branches gave birth to flowers,
Full of color, beautiful in every unique way.

And the flowers often became fruit,
That fed those around,
Juicy, succulent, life-giving.

And the seeds of the fruit, in the right time,
Fell to the earth and the dance of life began again.

This is the cycle of life: birth, inner knowing for growing up and
out, giving forth with beautiful expressions of life for us and others,
culminating in leaving our legacy when the seeds fall back to earth to
let life begin again.

There is no instruction book, no program to teach life to
live. Life just knows. That is the miracle, and that makes it all so
sacred.

We want to live. Living things want to live. Living things want to
grow.

It was that wanting to grow that got me off my knees many times in my life. I always knew life was precious, and I wanted more of it. So, I got up from fear, despair, and sadness.

I got up so I could find the joy.

This is my story of being born, growing up, giving out in the world, and letting go of seeds to be planted again for life to continue. I am still in my body, so I know I have more life to live and more to give forth.

Let's start at the beginning. Let me share the sacredness of life that I have come to learn about as I have lived my life.

PART ONE

The soil we grow up in matters,
for it informs how we grow.

The Soil I Grew Up In

As my mother would often say, "Something doesn't come from nothing." There must be a starting place, a foundation on which to stand. My life stands on the foundation of my parents and family, past and present. Their experiences flow through my veins, literally, as I carry their DNA. I also carry the energy of their gifts and tribulations.

Somewhere in me live the stories of my ancestors: the joys of family holidays in Poland; the feeling of hard work that my great-grandfather experienced as he ferried people, carts, and animals across rivers in Poland; the excitement of young men being able to study and learn at university; the women who were healers; the terror of being attacked by Cossacks because of their religion and way of life; the courage to leave a hostile environment to find a safer place to live and thrive.

All of those experiences live in me. I am made up of that. It doesn't mean that is all I am, but it is part of me. I come from a mixture of strong, resilient people and people full of weaknesses and imperfections. I come from something, not nothing. We all do.

I was born on a snowy, wintery Thanksgiving morning in November 1950, in Passaic, New Jersey to Ruth Shapiro and Jacob Groman. I love knowing I was born on Thanksgiving Day because of the theme of thankfulness and gratitude. At least, that is what the holiday means to me. Every few years, my birthday lands on Thanksgiving Day. Powerful, right? Yes.

Equally powerful is that the story of my birth, as remembered by my father, goes like this, "The day Vida was born, eighty-seven people died in a train crash on Long Island." One could read so much into that. I used to laugh at my dad when he told people that, but inside, my heart ached because he never said he was thrilled to have a second daughter who was born on Thanksgiving Day. Instead, he focused on what wasn't there anymore; he focused on death. That set the stage for growing up in the house of Groman.

Jack Groman

He never got to live, really live. The odds were against him. Growing up poor in Bronx, New York during the depression, there were days his family didn't have any food to eat. He and my grandmother would sometimes stand on street corners trying to sell little things just to get some money to buy food. His father, Isadore, unable to make a living for his family during the depression, opted out altogether and hung himself in the entrance hallway of their apartment when my father was thirteen years old. My father, his younger brother, and their mother came home to find Isadore Groman hanging. My grandmother, Lena, watched as her young sons cut down her husband. The three of them had to find a way to carry on and live. They developed a strength that allowed life.

Lena had her own struggles and torments that helped her grow her steel-like survival instincts. She'd come from Poland in the early 1900s to make money to bring her three brothers to the United States. It's the same story that immigrants from other countries have told over and over again: to better themselves, to be safe, to find a place to be free to live as they wanted to live. The courage that must have taken!

Lena worked in New York City and saved her money. She lived with the hope that she could save her family from the growing hatred in Poland. We are Jewish, so safety was central for our survival. Her hope vanished in the wind when her money was stolen. None of the brothers ever came over; instead, they grew up in Poland and had families. The 1930s arrived and the ghettos were created in many cities in Poland to imprison the Jews. Lena's family were all killed in that horrid, very real place called the Warsaw Ghetto.

Lena had survivor's guilt. She lived to seventy-five, but was emotionally distant and critical. Her heart seemed closed. I was basically terrified of her. When she stayed at our house for a week, I stayed as far away from her as possible. To be honest, the only memory of her that I love is that she could peel an apple in one continuous piece. I have tried and tried, but to this day, the peel always breaks somewhere before I have completed the process.

There were many strikes against Jack. Security, finances, and emotions were foreign experiences for him. He grew up in fear, sorrow, guilt, and loneliness. He tried to be a good son and he worked hard. As he was very smart, Jack went to Cornell University in upstate New York because they had a very good school of veterinary science. My dad loved animals. He wanted to become a veterinarian but didn't get accepted. Not because he wasn't smart enough, there were many scholars on my dad's side of my family, but because there was a quota for Jews and the quota was filled. He never became what he wanted to be most, settling instead for becoming a science teacher in the New York City school system.

While on leave from the army in 1946, he met my mother, Ruth Shapiro, at a party in upstate New Jersey. That night, my dad called his mother to tell her he had met the woman he wanted to marry. Three months later, they wed. Michele and I were born in the next few years. The story goes that my father wanted two sons, David and Michael. His daughters' names are Michele (the feminine of Michael) and Vida (the feminine of David).

On the surface, my dad was always uptight, frightened, and explosive. Under that top layer lived a very sensitive man. By the time

I knew my dad, he wouldn't drive a car. It was not that he couldn't, as he had a license, but many years earlier, he'd killed a cat while driving. That act bothered him so deeply he just couldn't get behind the wheel ever again. We had to take buses everywhere, which seems environmentally sound now, but back in my childhood, I felt so angry that we couldn't take "road trips" or "Sunday drives" the way my friends could. But to my dad, animals were special. I don't know how he came to that stance in life, but he did. We had box turtles, ducklings, cats, parakeets, and more. If he couldn't be a veterinarian, he was going to bring animals into our home, much to Mom's deep distress. Dad would have been a farmer if my mom hadn't put her foot down. That was the sensitive side of dad.

The top layer, though, won out more often than not after his mother died while visiting us. I remember it so well because Lena's death was a great turning point for our family, and for my life. My dad lost it after Lena died. The doctors told us he had experienced a nervous breakdown. Call it whatever you want, we basically lost my dad for decades. He just seemed to crack open and give up. Ten years old when that happened, I didn't know what was going on. I saw my dad crying, curled up on the living room floor and calling out for his mother. He was inconsolable, as if a part of him had died with her. The grief and terror of being without his mother consumed him immediately, so much so that Mom had to go to the funeral without him. Years later, when my mom died, my sister and I made the arrangements for her funeral without him as well. He just couldn't face it.

Growing up in the House of Groman became very challenging from that event forward. Dad's fears and anger became amplified. Never a big talker, Dad was a big observer, quietly watching others. But as his fears and anger grew, he became lost in his own mind and oblivious to us. I asked him, one time, what he was thinking. I wanted to know why he was always muttering to himself with his eyes closed, arm over his eyes, as he laid on the couch all day. He said he was seeing horrible movies in his head. At ten years old, none of that made sense to me. I just knew my dad was not there and I became scared.

My mother told me to humor him. "Don't fight with him," she said. I tried telling him jokes. I can picture him lying there in the living room, hand over those eyes once again. He never opened them. He just said, "I know what you're trying to do. I tried with my father, but he hung himself anyway."

We lived in New Jersey, and my dad had to get up at 5:30 a.m. every school day to take the bus to New York, then take subways to get to the high school where he taught. My mom had to drive him to the bus. He got home at 7:30 at night, when my mom picked him up from the bus station. After his mother died, I was awakened every morning by the sound of my dad retching in the bathroom. Then I would hear through his sobs, "I don't want to go." Like a child crying to his mother, but it wasn't his mother. It was his wife, my mother, who'd say, "Then don't go, Jack. What do you want from me?" Then he would go to work. After many years, he'd had enough and just stopped going to work. Dad took early retirement.

The years that followed were hard, plain and simple. Dad was either on the couch or raging over this thing or that. As I said, he was a quiet man who spoke little, but that didn't mean his insides were calm. He was always worried about something, or angry, or both. My mother thought yelling at him to "be a man" would get his juices going enough that he'd pop out of the trance of his internal horror to be "normal." Instead, Dad just got angrier and would lash out at me.

Dad would never hit my mother, so it was either my sister or me.

My sister kept quiet or found ways to go out with friends, and then her boyfriend, who later became her husband. Feeling some kind of loyalty to my mother, I would stay to protect her. I thought that was my job.

I was not quiet. I would speak up about my dad's controlling behavior toward my mother. For instance, when my mother, who was very social, went outside to talk to neighbors, my dad would time her. When he felt she'd been outside too long, he'd go out there and get her to come inside. The more I spoke up, the more he would explode. It didn't happen that often. The hard part was that I never knew when the explosion might occur. I learned to pay attention, to watch his arm to see if he might raise it to come down on me.

I hated him. I admit that. I am not proud of that feeling, but it is the truth. I didn't understand him and had no room or capacity for compassion at that time in my life. And I worried about my mother's health, all the time. She was tense, lonely, and felt like she had no power.

And so it went on, year after year. Time passes though. As humans, we either find a way to survive hardship or we don't and we can't go on. Each member of my family found their way forward. My sister got married, and I left New Jersey and moved to Wisconsin to go to graduate school in counseling. My parents, inching their way toward their senior years, moved to Florida, where my father began a landscaping business. Before his nervous breakdown, he'd loved gardening and had a small landscaping business In New Jersey. In Florida, he soon had plenty of work. He did the heavy lifting, planting trees and shrubs, and digging up old dead growth, while my mother made things look beautiful. She had an eye for beauty. They worked together and they worked hard.

It seemed that if my mother was by his side, he managed his anxieties and anger to some degree. He still spent time on the couch, arm over his eyes, caught in his internal movies, but getting outside and using his hands and body were a salve for his wounds. Doing made sense to him as it was real and practical, but making friends didn't. Although my mother had friends, she still couldn't spend much time with them before Dad would call her in.

As his psychiatrist said to him one time, "Jack, you will be fine as long as Ruth is alive." My mother couldn't keep that contract. She couldn't live forever. In 1987, my mother got sick. Three weeks after her diagnosis of cancer, she died.

Jack was on his own. My sister and I were left with the caretaking of a father we would rather not take care of. At least that was how I felt. We were dealing with losing our mother at a relatively young age (forty for my sister, thirty-seven for me). Our father was seventy-one. I was very close to my mother and needed time to grieve. Also, Dad lived in Florida, Michele in New Jersey, and I lived in Wisconsin. There was a lot to figure out. Lots to feel. Lots to manage.

My dad remarried a year after Mom died. He met Sylvia because his friend, Benny (his only friend), told him to write a letter to go in the local Jewish newspaper saying he was looking to meet someone. Sylvia responded to his letter. He married Sylvia, not because he loved her. No, he didn't. But above all things, my dad was practical. He needed someone to drive him places. Sylvia drove. End of story. They stayed together for the next eighteen years. My sister and I, as well as Sylvia's children, were beyond thrilled that they had found each other. Not because it was a good match, but because both were very difficult people to live with. We exchanged many stories of the pain of growing up with our respective parents.

Sylvia was incredibly verbally abusive, but my father didn't fight back. Whenever I visited and Sylvia began yelling, he would rush toward me and say, "Don't upset her. I will only have to hear about it after you leave."

After eighteen years, my dad called my sister and cried, "Come get me. Get me out of here." My brother-in-law hopped on a plane, packed a suitcase for my dad and off he went, back to New Jersey. He never spoke to Sylvia again. He never got divorced. He just moved forward, put pictures of my mother on his walls in his assisted living room and didn't look back.

Dad lived for another ten years in New Jersey, with my sister as his main support. I spoke to him often on the phone. Often, I would ask what he was watching on TV and then put that station on in my own home and we would watch a movie together. Sometimes, I'd call him when I was hiking or walking in the woods and tell him what I saw or ask him the name of a plant or tree. He could often tell me just by my description.

Those final years were a mixture of old arguments and newfound tenderness with him. The tenderness began during a phone call when my dad asked, "Was I a good dad?"

The question took my breath away. Was he a good dad? I breathed deeply. What was I going to say? I didn't want to destroy him. I would have, back in my younger days, but I was in my late fifties then. I had lived enough life to know that we all do the best that we know how to. I understood that if we knew better, we would do better. I decided to tell the truth, with love. I told him I wasn't going to lie, that he wasn't an easy person to grow up with. But, given all he'd experienced in his childhood, I believed he gave me the best he had. He cried and said, "There are so many things I wish I had done differently, Vida."

I knew he truly was asking me to forgive him for all of the hurtful words he'd said to me, for all the slaps and physical pain he'd caused me and my family. He was atoning for his actions. Love flowed in my heart. In that moment, I finally had a dad.

After that, Dad softened toward me and we had more intimate conversations. Don't get me wrong, we still fought on the phone. I once told him he was the most negative person I knew. He said, "I am not going to change," and I replied, with a laugh, "Dad, that is abundantly clear."

At one point, I decided that since he never said he loved me, I was going to teach him how and when to say it to me. Here's how the lesson went… Dad and I would talk about something meaningful, and I would say, "Dad, this would be a good time to say, 'I love you,' to me." It took a few times of coaching him – then he got it. Even if we had an argument, he would wait and say, "Shouldn't we say we love each other now?" Those were precious moments for me.

I so deeply appreciate that Invisible Choreographer we call God, Spirit, or the Divine for letting my dad live long enough for us to reach that point. What a journey from a train crash of a birth to the moment of saying, "I love you," even after an argument. This journey took many decades, but I can honestly say today, "I love my dad." I know he was not perfect, and I know he gave me the best he knew how to give.

My dad died in 2016 at the age of ninety-eight. He was eating in the dining room of his assisted living facility at the time. His table mates said he just keeled over at the table while chewing. I remember receiving the news. There was a knock on the door of my apartment. I was in the middle of a counseling session with a client, but something told me to get the door, so I excused myself. A dear friend was standing there, saying she needed to talk to me. I told her I would meet her after my session was over, not suspecting anything was wrong. When I met her, she told me my sister had called her because she couldn't reach me directly. "Vida, your father died earlier today." I heard the words and dropped to the floor, stunned and crying. In that moment, all the hurts, arguments, physical abuse, and sorrow washed away. My dad was dead.

Two days later, I was in New Jersey for the graveside service. Dad's body was buried next to my mother. It was a hot day in July. I remember worrying if I would be able to stand in the heat for long. I hate the heat. Few people came as Dad didn't have friends. So, it was me, my sister and her family, the remaining members of my mother's family and a few of my sister's friends. Before the ceremony began, we were standing on the road near the burial site when I turned and saw Dad's coffin being brought over to the open site. I broke down and cried. It was real.

The rabbi performed the Jewish service. I had asked him for time to speak about my dad. No one else would. I couldn't let my dad be buried without some words about him being said. I was shaking up and down the core of my being. I hadn't prepared anything the way I had when my mother died. I stood up, breathed, cried, and breathed again. Through my tears, I said, "These tears are not so much for Dad's passing as they are for his life not fully lived."

My Sacred Enemy

My dad was my greatest teacher. Some might say he was my Sacred Enemy – someone in life who seems like the enemy on the surface, but underneath, they are here to teach you deep lessons about life. Dad had many lessons to teach me.

His favorite saying was, "Let me tell you the worst that is going to happen." Yes, it might have saved him at times to be so prepared for the worst, but really, the worst that could happen! That was Dad, always looking for the negative. What a contrast for me – he named me Vida, Beloved Life, yet his lessons were around death, fear, limitation, and holding back. In other words, his lessons were about not living fully.

I watched my dad not live. The result was that a deep yearning to live life began to grow in my heart and soul. I remember when I was in my late teens and the bedroom I had shared with my sister since early childhood became mine. She got married and, of course, moved out of the house. My bedroom. Mine to decorate. Mine to spread out my energy into every corner of the room. It was seven years after my dad had had his nervous breakdown. During those years, I observed the landscape of life with a parent who was emotionally unhinged.

To get away from the drama and tension of my parents, I spent many hours alone in my bedroom. Of course, just being a teenager explains some of that alone time. In that private space, I'd ponder the meaning of life. I needed to know if what I was experiencing – the emotional pain, the arguing, the threats of suicide on my dad's part – was all there was to living. When I was ten years old, a counselor at our summer camp gave me a copy of *The Prophet*. She and I took walks and talked about the different writings from that amazing book. I learned about love; about what was possible. Added to that were my years of listening to folk music, to words and music that opened me up to social justice and injustice.

My ponderings were of deeper and higher thoughts. What was being played out around me was so different and painful from what I imagined was possible, from being exposed to new thoughts and ways of being in the world. To remind myself of how I wanted to live, I posted a piece of paper on the wall next to my bed. It said:

The essence of life is to live it fully.

I was seventeen when I wrote that message to myself.

When I ask myself what I learned from growing up with Jack, I answer, "Jack taught me that it matters that I live alive." I was given what was mine in life. Then I got to decide if I was going to resist it, argue with it or be open to it. I got to decide if I was going to be curious about it, wonder about it and find what was important for me to learn so I could live fully.

*Living alive is being open to feeling what I
feel, speaking my truth, opening my heart
and allowing the full range of emotions to
move through me.*

Jack's life taught me to grow my compassion, to open my heart to that which hurts so badly. My heart would not have cracked open or grown to her depths without my journey with my dad. I know so deeply now that I want to live my life with an open heart. In spite of it not being easy, or perhaps because of that, I learned that I wanted to live my life as a human expression of Spirit. My dad was not willing to feel. He shut himself off from Spirit. Every time he felt an intense emotion, he wanted his antipsychotic meds. I would say to him, "Dad, it's only an emotion. Just breathe." He would say, "No, just get my meds." He had no time for emotions or God in any form.

Sometimes our teacher leads us toward something. Sometimes our teacher leads us by showing us how not to live. My dad was the latter kind of teacher. His teachings were still profoundly powerful for me. My lessons learned so early through living in the House of Groman deeply affected every aspect of my life going forward. I am indeed grateful for my dad. He taught me about the love of animals and nature, about humility, and compassion. My father taught me to love again, even after the hurt. I truly can say, "I love you, Dad." And mostly, he taught me how sacred life is and that life asks that we live it fully.

Amen.

So it is.

Ruth Groman, nee Shapiro

I remember the last time I sat with my mother. For three weeks after her diagnosis of cancer, my sister and I were with her at the hospital, all day, every day. Mom had been in a coma for the past few days and her body was swollen and moist, which is what happens when the body fills up with fluid. It is called ascites.

Earlier that day, the nurse had told us Mom would probably pass that night. For reasons I don't fully understand, I agreed to go home instead of staying. Maybe it was fear, maybe denial, since the nurse had told us for the past three days that Mom might die that night and there she was, alive the next day. Michele and I felt strongly that we needed to say goodbye to our mother separately, just in case the nurse was right. My sister went first. It was then that I really understood how each child has their own unique relationship with that parent. Unique and private.

I waited for Michele to come out. My heart beating quickly, tears flowing down my cheeks, I wondered what I would say to this woman I called Mom. I loved her so much. The door opened and out walked my sister, her eyes wet, her body bent forward with sorrow. Now it was my turn. I walked in, sat down, and leaned over to kiss her forehead. My lips touched moist, cool skin. As I breathed deeply, I prayed for guidance. My hand rose, as if by magic, and I gently reached for her hand. Her breath was labored.

My words came forth, "Mom, thank you for giving birth to me, for laboring to push me out into the world." I thanked her for loving me, for teaching me about heart and humor. I told her how I planned on using what she gave me in my work with others. "You mattered," I said. I reminded her to look for her mother and the rest of her family. One last time, I leaned over to kiss her forehead. Then I walked out.

At my mother's funeral service in New Jersey, I stood behind her closed, plain wooden casket in front of a small group of family and friends. A few moments before, my sister Michele, my Aunt Ida (my mother's sister) and I had gathered in another room to tear the piece of cloth the rabbi had pinned to our clothes. It is a Jewish tradition to tear your clothes as a way of showing the tear in your heart over a loved one lost. We each tore the pinned black cloth for the one to the left of us. My Aunt Ida, who was older than my mother, began to lose her balance in her grief. Michele and I reached for her and the three of us were one. We regained our composure and walked into the room where the service was being held.

It was 1987 and I was thirty-seven years old. I was the only one who got up to speak about her. The rabbi, a Cohen, was in the hallway, conducting the service via microphone. In ancient Jewish history, Cohens were the high priests of the temple and were not allowed to be near dead bodies. So, he was in the hallway. I had never met him before, but he looked like every image I have ever had about a European rabbi. He was old, with white hair on his head and a long white beard. I had called him to ask when I could speak about my mother. I didn't ask if, just when. Graciously, and with a beautiful, old country Jewish accent, he said, "This is the best time for you to speak." I thanked him. The words I wanted to share had come to me two hours before the service. I had told my sister to leave me alone for a while, then the words flowed through me. I swear the words were not from me. Fifteen minutes after I started writing, it was complete.

As I stood behind the casket, I could see my sister crying in the front row. I am very close to my sister and my heart ached for her. My heart ached for me. There was a religious cloth draped over the pine box. I placed a photograph of Mom on that cloth, along with the piece of paper with the words that had come through.

My mother's funeral was the first funeral I had ever been to.

Silence. I breathed, then began reading.

Years later, in 2016, I auditioned and was selected to be among a small group of writers to read a piece about mothers and mothering. The show, called *Listen to Your Mother,* was created annually by Ann Imig in Madison. *Listen to Your Mother* expanded nationwide and into Canada. I knew I had to be part of that show. The core of my piece was what I had written the day my mother died. In twenty minutes, I wrote the introduction to it. I thank Ann Imig every day of my life for that experience. It was the first time I had ever stood in front of an audience that large. It was also the first time I had ever read what I'd written in front of people I didn't know!

Let me begin my sharing of my mother by sharing the piece I read in front of 500 people on July 14, 2016.

My Mother's Name Was Ruthie

My mother's name was Ruthie. Really it was
Ruth, Ruth Shapiro before she married my father.
My sister and I just loved to call her Ruthie.
Actually, we liked to call her Maw, which sounds
so wrong right now, or Moo when she brought us
our milk. We thought that was funny. She would

get annoyed. She liked being called "Mom" the best. I still refer to her as Ruthie.

My mother's name was Ruthie. She used to get out of the shower with a towel wrapped around her large body and come into our bedroom doing a little dance for us. My sister and I would bend over and laugh hysterically, both loving our mother's silliness and majorly amazed she could be so ridiculous.

My mother's name was Ruthie. She loved connecting with people. My father didn't. One year, my parents came to visit me. They had taken the train up from Florida because my father was afraid to fly. When I picked them up at the Chicago train station, I noticed my father seemed so upset with my mother. I asked him what was wrong and he told me my mother had told everyone everything about our family. My mother quickly replied, "Oh, Jack, what do you want from me. They said hello. What else was I to do?"

My mother's name was Ruthie. She came from a little village in Poland called Kobrin. When she was several years old, there was a Pogrom, a raid of the village by government soldiers. My mother's family escaped to Danzig, Germany, where, because she was very ill at the time, the captain of the ship bound for the United States had to be bribed to let my mother on board. But they made it, and Passaic, New Jersey became home to my mother. That is where she grew up, and where her mother died when she was eleven. She had many boyfriends, and several marriage proposals. Ruthie said no to all of them and then met my father. They married because her family convinced her she was getting old at thirty-three, she needed to get married, and besides, his family was nice. Then my sister Michele and I came along. My mother's life with my father was very difficult and lonely. Sometimes Michele and I would ask why she married him.

My mother's name was Ruthie. In 1987 I got a phone call saying I needed to come to Florida. Mom was sick. We took her to the doctor. She had cancer. The doctors kept referring to her as "patients like that." I told them, "Our mother's name is Ruth and you will call her by her name." The nurses clapped silently behind the doctors. The night before the surgery, I remember my last walk with my mother. My sister was on her left, I was on her right, and we went walking down the corridor. A man was walking alongside us. He looked at us and asked my mother who "these beautiful young women" were. Without missing a beat, she turned and said to him, "These are my pride and joy." I never felt my heart so full.

On February 26th at 10:23 a.m. we received the call that our mother had died. Ruthie was gone. We flew her body up to Passaic, New Jersey, where she was to be buried.

This is the Blessing I wrote for my mother:

A Blessing for Ruthie

From your loins I sprang,
Fearful to take my stand in this life.
But I looked up and saw you laying there
pushing,
Bearing me forth to this life,
to live this life.

This I did learn from you, Ruthie,
To live this life with curiosity, gusto,
and deep-rooted joy, spreading compassion and
love.

This I did learn from you, Ruthie,
To accept with surrender and strength what
comes,
to cry at the drop of a hat from the bottom of my
heart, did I learn.

To speak with the truth and a story,
Like none I've ever heard before,
Did I learn from you, Ruthie.

I grew strong and straight, not so straight,
And your love fortified me to stretch and reach,
For what I know not, and reach I did,
Till I pass over to meet you and be with you
(and yes, Mama, I do know for what I reach).

I have a love so deep for you, Ruthie, that will last
the ages,
For you are and will always be my mother, my
compassion, my strength, my guidance, and I do
love you.
I dedicate my life to living and teaching others to
live with love, compassion and wisdom in your
name, Ruthie,
and I cry for joy that I know you.
I will miss only your body, for your spirit will be
with me always. HO!

Ruthie was the one I turned to whenever I was scared or lonely. I turned to her when I wanted to share the goods things as well. She was my go-to gal, and my refuge in a tornadic family dynamic of pain.

I was a very sensitive child, easily upset by other people's emotions. Sometimes, I would lie awake for hours in my bed, worrying about some person or event that didn't go well, while my sister slept soundly in her bed next to me. After hours of being in torment with my own young mind, I would get up and walk slowly to my parents' bedroom. The door was always closed, so I had to find my courage to knock. "Mom, Mom, I can't sleep." I hated those few moments, wondering if I would get yelled at for waking them up. Then I would hear my mother say, "Come in, Vida." My father would turn away from us and complain, "What does she want?" but my mother would just tell him to go back to sleep. I would then sit at the edge of the bed, crying, while she rubbed my back and tried to soothe me with her words. I always felt relief. Then I would go back to my room and sleep the sleep of being safe and loved.

Ruthie could be sarcastic. We were both hands-on kind of women and loved doing craft projects together. One year, when I was still living at home, we wallpapered my bedroom. Neither of us knew what we were doing, but we bought the supplies, talked with the guy at the store, and started. When we were nearly done, my father came in. He walked around looking at the walls and found a slight imperfection, a lump in one spot. "You've got a spot here that isn't right." He kept rubbing his finger on that spot over and over again. My mother turned to him and said, "Go ahead, Jack. Keep rubbing it. Maybe it will go away."

She also thought she had the corner on how to do things right. When we worked on a project together and I would do the next step, she would jump in and say, "Let me show you the right way to do that." I am my mother's daughter, so sarcasm lives in me as well. "You mean your way, Mom?" We would both laugh and carry on.

Ruthie taught me about relationships and how to connect with other people. My parents visited me in Wisconsin one summertime, where I was living with my boyfriend in the new house we'd bought. It had a tiny postage stamp of a backyard, where the previous owners had planted several fruit trees, strawberry patches, and other wonderful flowers. Mom went out to look around and see what she could do to help us. All of a sudden, she came in and said, "Get ready to go to Mrs. Troia's house for tea and cake." I asked, "Who was Mrs. Troia?" We had just moved in, so we didn't know anyone at the time. Mom said she was my neighbor from around the corner behind our house.

Apparently, Mom had struck up a conversation with Mrs. Troia out in the yard, over the fence. In the short time Mom was out there, they had exchanged cut flowers from each other's yards and Mrs. Troia had invited both of us over to eat the cake she'd just baked. There you are – a Ruthie moment.

The years living with my dad eventually took their toll on her. She became more impatient, nervous, and tired. Her words could be cruel at times. We were never a religious family. My father didn't believe in any higher power, and it was never clear to me what my mom believed. She would have liked to belong to a Temple for the community and connection, but I never heard her talk about faith.

When I was twenty-nine years old, I began my spiritual journey. I wanted to share with her what I was discovering from my readings and meditation experience. I took a chance and shared what had deep meaning to me. My mom's reply, "What did you go and do, Vida? Suddenly discover God?" landed in my heart like a hard slap. I turned to her and said, "I guess I have, Mom." That was the end of that. I believe by that time she was worn out. Her heart was closing to life.

When Mom died at age seventy-four, Michele and I told each other that she got tired and didn't know any other way to leave my dad.

My Mother's Family

Schmuel (Samuel) and Chaya Turnunsky, my great-grandparents, lived in a small town in what is now Poland, but at the time was probably the Ukraine or Belarus. My grandmother was one of seven Turnunsky children: three girls, four boys. My mother's family escaped in the early 1900s to come to America. My grandmother, Minnie (Mindel in Yiddish) and her sister, Freida (Frumi in Yiddish) moved with their families to the New Jersey area. My grandmother and my great aunt were very close. My Aunt Frieda would never leave her sister. Freida's husband, Sholom, had relatives in the New Jersey area, so North it was.

My great aunt Florence, great uncles Morris, Edward, Hyman, and Meyer landed in Mississippi. Family had settled there earlier in the century. I never really knew my southern relatives. Their only influence on me consisted of me choosing to do a report in 4th grade on Mississippi. Through my research about the state and my relatives, I learned the family name was shortened to Turner upon their arrival at Ellis Island in the early 1900s. In Webb, Mississippi, my uncles had a department store called Turner Bros.

Florence came north when I was a little girl. The only thing I remember about her was that she spoke Yiddish with a Southern accent. Of course, that sounded weird to my ears as I was accustomed to hearing Yiddish with a Northern accent. Who knew "Oy Vey" could sound so different. My mother, Aunt Ida, and Tonta Frumi still spoke Yiddish to each other when they wanted to hide something from the children, or my father, who only spoke English.

I never knew my grandmother, Mindel, as she died at thirty-six of ovarian cancer. When I saw a photo of her, I thought she was in her sixties because she looked so worn out and old. My Tonta Frumi stepped in to take care of my mother until my grandfather, Joseph Shapiro, remarried. He died when I was four years old, so I have no memories of him. He married a widow with a young son and they had two sons together, my mother's half-brothers.

Life with my grandfather and his second wife was unbearable for my mother because the sons were favored over the daughters, and because the second Mrs. Shapiro was just plain nasty to my mother. The best foods were given to the boys. Milk came in bottles with the cream riding on top of the skimmed milk. Cream was considered to be the best food, so the boys had milk mixed with the cream. My mother just had the skimmed milk. At that time, the best or healthy foods were different from what we know now. The message was that boys were supreme and girls were less than boys.

In her late teens, my mother decided to leave her family to live with Tonta Frumi. She couldn't say she was leaving as that would be going against the wishes of her father. Instead, every day, she would wear layers of her clothes to go to work and then leave pieces of her wardrobe at my Tonta's house. When she had cleaned out her closet, she left and never went back. I have tried to imagine my mother with layers of clothes on her body, sneaking around so she could gain her freedom. My mother was braver than I realized – she was committed to her freedom.

By the time my sister and I arrived on the scene, Tonta Frumi was our grandmother. My family would visit her and her husband, my uncle Sholom, a fruit peddler who used to sell vegetables and fruit from his horse-drawn wagon. Sholom, which means peace in Yiddish, lived up to his name. I can't remember Sholom ever engaging in a full conversation. He was a doer and a listener, not a talker. Tonta Frumi was just the opposite, a talker. She and my mother would chatter away, half in Yiddish, half in English. I loved listening to them. I didn't understand Yiddish. I didn't have to. I just needed to wait for those English words that came out whenever Yiddish did not cover that part of the sentence and I got the gist. I would hear my mother and aunt talking in Yiddish and more Yiddish and would hear the word "children" in English. I knew my sister and I were either in trouble or, let's face it, more often than not, we were in trouble. The trouble always seemed so much more intense when told in another language.

My most warmhearted memory about Tonta Frumi was the time my mother and I had a screaming match at my aunt's house. I was in my teens then, so fights were common. Mom won. I was crying and feeling miserable. Tonta came over to me and put her arms around my shoulders, pulling my head to her breast. One of my ears was pressed to her body, but I could still hear with my open ear. What I heard was my Tonta's soft, tender Eastern European accent, "Sha, Sha Mamala. It's going to be alright. Sha, Sha, I am here."

And then she would do what she always did. She made me a glass of hot tea; not a cup, a glass of hot tea. She would get two glasses, heat the water, and when the water was hot enough, she would fill one of the glasses. Into that glass went the tea bag, along with a "titch" of sweet syrup. Then Tonta would pour the hot brew from one glass to the other, back and forth, to cool the temperature down. When the tea was at just the right temperature, she handed me the glass to drink. It always soothed me. Did I say that I loved Tonta Frumi? I loved her very much.

That story has always stayed with me. Recently, I was working with a woman in a healing session and there came a moment where self-love was needed. The tea memory came to mind. As I often do, I let myself share this story with my client. I invited her to imagine the "Tonta Frumi" holding her to her own breast, then invited her to say words of comfort to herself. She did. She cried. I invited her to make tea with a "titch" of sweet syrup and get two glasses so she could pour the tea back and forth until the temperature was just right. She promised she would.

Tonta Frumi was one of my best teachers. I learned about love and tenderness and how to prepare and drink sweet tea to soothe my heart and soul.

You now know about the soil I grew up in. My people are a mixture of tenderness, sensitivity, intellect, harshness, and cruelty. There was love. There was hurt. I have learned I must be willing to acknowledge all of it. Not to dwell on it, but to know where I come from. There are gifts in what my family gave to me. They survived, and some thrived. I survived and I chose to thrive. I was planted in this soil. And I grew. I am proud to know I come from scholars and ferrymen. I come from cantors and department store owners. I come from strong women who raised children, embraced grandchildren, created art, and stood up for social justice. In writing about my family, I have come full circle back to them, to reclaim my roots. I know they were far from perfect. I accept that and, in that acceptance, I am finding I am accepting myself more and more.

I feel like I am meeting myself in new ways, like I just found myself as I turned the corner. And I stand before me and say, "I am here. Sha, Sha. It is all alright. Let's drink tea. Let's walk together into our next steps of living."

PART TWO

Having been nourished by the soil,
the seed grows forward and reaches for the light.
It's in its nature.

It's is in our nature.

Seed Growing Forward

Seeds in the ground know just when to break through the encasement that holds them in. That encasement, at first, keeps the seed, the potential for life, safe. But there comes a time when that potential, the "thing" that it's supposed to be, needs to crack through the binds and walk out into the life that it is. That's true for a seed. That's true for every human.

A seed grows in the soil it was planted in and must find its way to literally grow up. That is what our childhood into early adulthood is about for humans, but our process is much slower and is filled with many pitfalls, opportunities to ask for help from others, moments of learning, and moments of forgetting. And grow we continue to do into our adult years. In all honesty, I believe seeds in the ground might have an easier time in this growing forward process than humans. As far as I know, seeds don't have to deal with a mind. Humans do. Heaven, help us! Please.

My seed broke open mostly through adversity. I know most people want to read about the high points in someone's life, about the celebrations and breakthroughs. So do I. Breakthroughs, though, mean so much more to me when I have the back story. When I can see what someone walked through and how they righted themselves, then I trust the gifts they bring to me more deeply.

When I reflect on my growing-up years, I need to be honest and say those years were hard. I was a sensitive, emotional child, born into a highly anxious and frightened family. I picked up on that energy early on. Later, the ability to perceive energy and emotions became one of my gifts in working with people, but that innate gift would be a liability for quite a while before I claimed it. I just knew folks around me were not happy. My world became one of hypervigilance, paying attention to the adults around me, trying to figure out what was needed, or how I could stay out of the way of the turmoil.

The defining year of my life that set the stage for how I felt about myself and what I created going forward was my tenth year. That year was a perfect storm. First, my life, my family changed forever when my grandmother, Dad's mom, died at our house. Dad then had his nervous breakdown, and I tore the cartilage in my left knee and was out of school for two months to heal.

My world had turned upside down, with no one to help me find my footing. It wasn't enough that my parents' focus was redirected from raising two daughters to making sure my father survived the death of his mother – the tension in the house was constant. We walked on eggshells so as not to upset my dad. His outbursts of anger that at times led to my getting hit was enough to disrupt my growing up, but I was also lifted out of my social world when I tore that cartilage.

It was a silly thing. My sister and I had a babysitting job across our street for friends of my parents. It was raining, and as we ran down the sidewalk, my foot hit a raised section and I fell onto my left knee. I remember the pain as my knee made contact with the concrete. I knew something big had happened inside my body.

As the doctor wrapped my entire leg with plaster, from groin to ankle, I realized I wouldn't be able to move around easily. And I was right – that cast was heavy! The answer was to keep me home for two months while my cartilage healed. That was awful for me. First, because I was a very physically active child and not being able to move made me feel like a prisoner in my own life, and more importantly, I was isolated from my friends. I was scared those friends would move on to find others to play with, and that is exactly what happened. I got left out.

All those events initially left me devastated. I felt alone within my own family and within my own friend circle. I had to learn how to adapt. And I did. In the years of my alone time, I learned how beautiful it was to walk in the woods, listening to the sounds of the wind blowing through the leaves above me. I learned the beauty of listening to classical and folk music, feeling their melodies moving through my body, soothing me. In those alone times, I connected deeply with myself, and I pondered the meaning of life.

It is amazing to notice that what starts as a survival response can turn into strengths later in life. I have always believed if I can survive the hard times, I can use what I have gone through to teach myself something. And then, I can share what I learned with others. The experience "wasn't for nothing." So, those years of feeling different from kids my age, those times of being alone, finding my way through hard emotions, became teaching lessons, albeit hard won.

Cat Love Saved Me

I have lived with cats for over sixty-five years. Each cat came with their unique personality and philosophy of life. My current feline companion is Bella, a Birman. She is also a princess. Bella moves through the world with elegance, grace, and an attitude that she is the center of it all. I am here to serve her. She is loving, affectionate, and clear about her boundaries. I know when I have crossed the line of too much touch. I love that about her. I know where I stand.

One of her predecessors was named Fluffy, a totally white, short-haired, blue-eyed female whose role in life was to be a mother, repeatedly. She gave birth to many kittens in her lifetime and mothering came easily to her. I benefited from her ability to love and comfort. When I was fifteen, my father and I had a huge fight. He had hit me across the head and I knew I needed to run for protection or I would feel the blows of his hands again.

I ran for the bathroom, and just as I was closing the door, Fluffy ran in with me. I sat on the edge of the tub, crying. Fluffy jumped up on the tub and began making the sounds a mother cat makes to soothe her kittens. It's not a meow, more like a short purr. Then she moved closer to me. I leaned over to her and she gave me a love bite on my cheek. It was gentle, like I'd seen her do to many of her kittens. Then she rubbed her face on mine. I knew I was loved.

As my father pounded on the door, screaming at me, my cat,

another species, made sure I knew I was safe and loved. She saved my soul that day. I don't think the comfort she gave me would have meant as much if it had come from my own species. Cats can't be made to love. They can't fake it. I knew her love was real. I knew I wasn't alone.

Where Did My Voice Go?

My best friend in my world was my cousin. Six months older than me, she lived downstairs in our two-story house and we often played together. One day, we were trying to figure out what we were going to do. Would it be playing under our homemade cave of tables and chairs covered by blankets in the basement, or playing ship on the side porch going into my cousin's kitchen?

My cousin was indecisive, so I took charge. She ended up crying. I don't know what I did to upset her. I loved my cousin and can't imagine intentionally hurting her, but there she was, my cousin, my best friend, upset. Her mother came running out to find her daughter in tears. I was severely reprimanded for being "bossy" and taking charge. My aunt never asked me or my cousin what happened. She just assumed I had done something to hurt her daughter. That was so painful for me that I made a promise to myself that I would never let my words hurt anyone ever again.

That decision to stifle my words colored my expression for decades. I would stop myself from speaking. When it would have been healthy for me to say no, I wouldn't, because I feared I might hurt someone. That day, I made the decision to not only stifle my voice, but unconsciously, to stifle my power. After all, in my child mind, my stepping into my power might hurt another human being and I couldn't live with myself if I did that.

Through the years, I have revisited that moment of choice that kept me small. The child in me held onto that energy, the belief that by being me, standing in my power, I could be dangerous. No one corrected my child thinking. One moment in time – long-term consequences in a life.

Later, I became the one to hold my child self and comfort that pain. I showed her how to use her power to be the kind of leader she wanted to be – the leader I really wanted to be.

Many years later, I had a vision about being a leader. On the horizon of a great desert, I saw a very tall being, dressed in a long robe. She was walking. Behind her, a long line of people, smaller in height, followed. There were no words, just silence. In my mind's eye, I watched the movement going forward. From somewhere beyond my mind, I was asked, "What makes a good leader?" I looked at that image and knew. The leader on the horizon walked fully in her body, centered. She was connected to her heart in her authenticity. The people behind her wanted to feel that way as well. That is why they were following her – to learn how to be embodied, fully, in their hearts and integrity.

I found my blueprint for leadership. I needed to become me. Fully. To be true to my heart and soul.

"You Are Too Intense," They Told Me

I have always wanted to connect with the depths of myself, to have the courage to travel to my inner worlds to shine the light on the secrets of my soul, make love to myself, partner with myself till the end of time. How can I explain that to anyone else? I was told as a child that I was too much, too intense, too sensitive, all the while being treated as if I were not enough. Too much, too little. What ground was I supposed to stand on with those contradictory messages being leveled at me? I used to wonder if anyone else felt that way, or was I the only one to feel that deeply, that much?

As a little girl, I used to go into the living room closet. In the corner of the room, it was where my dad hung his clothes. It was also the place where my parents kept the record player. In the record cabinet were LPs of classical music my cousin, Adolph, had given us. I'd put my small rocking chair in there and sit and listen to those records. Rocking back and forth, light shining from a window in the closet, I would let the music wash over me, touching my soul. Eyes closed; I'd feel the drama of the music as it took me to the lithe spirits of nature. Each recording had its own rhythm and tenor and took me to a different journey within. My own worlds, private and deep, each one a full experience that widened me, that grew my heart and soul. How in God's name could I share that with anyone else?

I always had so much intensity of emotion and sensation in my body. I just couldn't find words to let others know what was going on inside me. A loner when I was young, not having to talk was so soothing and comfortable for me. Give me a box filled with pieces of a plastic bird to glue together, leave me alone for hours so I could paint by numbers or teach myself how to read music by making up my own system so I could play the plastic flute. Create space in my basement for me to put together the Visible Man, an amazing kit for learning about the human body systems. And the ultimate – putting together the Visible Woman, complete with the pregnant version of her. I was in heaven. Seeing, doing, creating; that was my world. It was safer. There weren't any conflicts. I oversaw what I did.

I had a much easier time seeing and doing. If I could be patient, the seeing and doing became words that came from a very deep place within me. To be clear, my learning process was not a learning disability at all. My words became sacred and precious once I understood how they developed in me. But that understanding didn't happen until I was well into my adult years.

There were many moments I wished I were somebody else as I listened to others being so articulate, while there I was moving my hands in the air, trying to find the right word to express the depth of feeling or knowing that lived within me. The unfortunate thing is I came to believe I was stupid, or at least not as smart as people I knew. After many years of trying to embrace the gifts of my mind, I have found such pleasure and excitement in how I process the world within and around me. I love that words are so precious to me and deep conversations are so intimate. I love that I need to move my body to know what I am thinking, and that my thinking comes in the form of feelings. I love that I love silence. I love that I am aware of both my feelings, and others' feelings, at the same time.

Teach Me How

My family started going to summer camp in 1954. My parents worked at the camp and my sister and I were campers there. I was only four years old at the time, much younger than the other little girls in my cabin who were at least five years old or older. My parents were busy during the day, so I never really saw them. I missed my mom terribly though, and by the evening I was inconsolable. Bedtime was a disaster. I would start crying as the sun went down and didn't stop until the counselor called my parents to come and say goodnight to me.

While waiting for my parents to arrive, I sat on my counselor's lap, tearing bits of tissue to roll into little balls and then dropping each one onto the floor. I now know that little kinesthetic action soothed me. By the time my parents showed up, there would be a pile of little white balls on the cabin floor.

To this day, I usually have a piece of torn paper rolled-up in my hand. It still soothes and centers me. Back then, I remember feeling so abandoned and scared. Even though there were other people around me, I felt so alone. Young children need to be encouraged to step out into the world to try new things, meet new people, and stretch their skills. They also need to run back and check in with their parent for security. They need to know they are not alone, that there is safety.

That running back to check in with Mom or Dad is called refueling. I now see it whenever I am watching young children at a park. They run off to play, then occasionally come running back to touch or talk to a parent, then off they go again, back into the world. I didn't have that going on at camp. In my young mind, I was on my own. To this day, whenever I remember that first year at camp, my stomach clenches and I feel such compassion for my little one.

Feeling alone and on my own became a theme for me as I grew up. School became another place where I was younger than everyone else and on my own. I started school at four-and-a-half years old. Somehow, my mother registered me early, so I began my education earlier than most children. Then in 4th grade, the New Jersey system changed from half-year promotions to full year and I was "promoted" an entire year. That meant I was even younger than the other kids in my new class.

I had no difficulty academically, but socially was a different situation. I was shy to begin with and my interests were already more internal and reflective. I guess I was quite precocious. At ten years old, I read *The Prophet* by Kahlil Gibran. My mind was focused on the meaning of life, not on boys or clothes. My choice of music was folk and not The Beatles. More and more, I found myself on my own, feeling different from those around me. Making friends was a puzzle for me. I never knew what to say to get started. My world was so internal and yet I was so lonely, so hungry for connection.

It pained my mother to see how much I was suffering. Gifted in making connections with others, she decided to take the time to teach me how to talk to other girls so I could have friends. As it turned out, her talking lessons were really gossip lessons. Not mean gossip, just how to talk about this one and that one with a friend on the phone. I learned quickly and well. Much to my mother's annoyance, I ended up on the phone every evening, talking away for hours. I am deeply grateful to her. She helped open doors for me to have friends. I learned how to have "lighter conversations." Now I could have both light and deep talks. This was one of the few times one of my parents taught me how to find my way through a difficult situation.

I started college at sixteen years old at Paterson State College in Wayne, New Jersey, and was at least two years younger than everyone else. In my freshman year, I had to take statistics. Let me be very clear, I hated anything to do with numbers. Let me study history, art, music, theater, and writing. My favorite thing was to take those classes from the same historical period. For example, Renaissance history, art, music, and theater classes at the same time. I loved how the arts enriched my knowledge of that historical time. I could see, feel, and hear the people.

Statistics didn't have that appeal for me. I couldn't feel it. There was nothing intuitive to reach out to. As the semester progressed, I didn't. I was close to failing the course. When I asked my father for help, his answer was to write a letter to the dean asking to be allowed to drop the class. In my shyness, it never occurred to me to talk to the instructor to get help. So, my only option, as my father convinced me, was to walk into the dean's office and hand her that note.

That is what I did. I can see her now, sitting behind her desk, letting me dig a hole so big I couldn't get out. After I'd said my piece and handed her the note, she looked at it. A note written in my father's handwriting, signed by my father. There was silence, then she leaned over her desk, "If you are not old enough to hack it here at college, drop out!"

That was it; no offer of help, no supportive language. I was sixteen and on my own. In a millisecond my response came out of my mouth, "Never mind. I am not going to drop out of the class. I don't care if I fail. I am staying." I walked out of the room, feeling humiliated and deeply betrayed by both my father and the dean. I passed the class because the professor marked us all on a curve. It seems I was surrounded by poets and artists. Most of us had little clue what statistics really meant. I do apologize to those of you who love mathematics and see the beauty in it. I bow to you with deep respect.

As I look back on those years, I realize how alone I felt. I so wished I could turn to my parents to learn how to be resilient. Learning how to be resilient teaches a child how to have faith in themselves. When an adult teaches a child how to move through challenging situations, the child learns confidence and develops trust in their self and in life. And most importantly, a child learns she can be safe in the world. I didn't get that, not from my parents. I suffered from the lack of being taught "how" in life.

But there is a gift within this story. A hunger grew in me. That hunger was for something better than what I was experiencing in my family. I knew there had to be something more than that. There had to be. I wanted to find the "something more" in life. That yearning led me to study anything I could find about higher meaning and purpose. I wanted to know about connection with myself and others. More profoundly, I wanted to know about connection with something invisible beyond my seeing, knowing there was so much more than I could see with my physical eyes.

I wrote a piece about that childhood yearning to connect with others.

> I sit now on a sidewalk curb.
>
> Birds singing within spaces of silence that trees make. The silence of growing deep and tall, all in a line. The line of what is natural.

I used to sit on the stoop of my house, as a young child, with a purpose. Not just to sit. I made it my purpose to say hello to everyone I met who was walking past our house. It was an experiment, you see. To see how people would respond to a stranger making contact. Honest, non-demanding contact.

Lives walking past a stoop. A small child saying, "Hi, Hello. How are you?"

Oh, I got some looks. Surprise, disdain, annoyance, but inside of me a deep calling was stirring. The calling to contact human life. To reach out and create a bond, an honest bond, even for a moment in time, an honest moment in time, to leave my soft, gentle whisper of a fingerprint in their heart.

So, my purpose, and the meaning of my life, started then.

And here I am, today, learning still about a smile, a nod, a bow, a recognition of someone else's light. And I am taken back to my childhood, after dinner when I used to run downstairs, sit on my stoop, and wait in silence for the passing contact with life.

And I smile.

My seed was growing forward, knowing I needed to find new soil that would nourish me and support me in finding out who I was so I could flourish and flower.

The pains and sorrows of my early years were not mistakes. No, not at all. My early years were an education of their own. I was given the experiences of "not having" so a hunger in me could grow into yearning, and that yearning could grow into commitment to living into my name – the name given to me by my father – Vida. It means Life, you know.

PART THREE

Reaching toward life,
branches grow stronger and flower.
May we reach for life.

Branches Reaching Out

I started having what I call "teaching dreams" in my early thirties – dreams where I am not fully asleep, and I know as I am dreaming that I am being given a message or a teaching to integrate into my daily life. The following is one such dream. I had been doubting myself for quite some time, not taking myself seriously. My guides must have been watching me struggle, so I was given this dream, full of visual, kinesthetic, and auditory imagery; a full sensory experience. The message has stayed with me for over thirty-five years. I am still learning how to live according to that message.

My Dream

A close up of my head. My hands over my ears. Mouths, only mouths, surround my head. Lips move as each mouth tells me what I should be doing, what I should be thinking, who I am. OMG! It is too much.

I run like a frightened rabbit away from the mouths. I run and I run, breathing heavily with each step. I don't know where I am going. I just run to get away from all those words. I feel so trapped. Running is my way out.

I run till I can't take another step. My legs almost give out. Each breath hard to find, I stand still. Silence. I hear nothing. I am alone with myself. Relief. Then I notice two Spirit Beings, one on each side of me. I feel a light pressure on each of my feet and realize each Being places their energy foot on mine. Within a moment, I feel energy moving so powerfully up my legs, into my belly, up my torso, and into my arms and head. My full body is filled with me. My energy. I stand more powerfully than I can ever remember.

In front of me, a disembodied voice said, "Now, Vida, are you ready to take yourself seriously?"

Being Me

When I imagine a tree, I start with what's under the ground, beneath what's visible. I can't see under the ground, but I know a seed has burst forth, growing roots down into the earth and spreading out in all directions. Nourishment comes to the tree through those roots; so much going on. We, who walk on the surface of the earth, aren't aware of any of this. Only when the trunk begins to break through can we know this is becoming a tree. And the trunk grows, always taking in what it receives from its roots and making something from it. Branches are part of that trunk, reaching up and spreading out in a mirror reflection of the roots beneath the surface. The invisible grows into the visible. The seed knows what it is. Nothing can make it grow into anything other than what it is meant to be. Something inside knows who it really is.

I once had a numerology reading. Numerology is based on the number of letters in your name. My name is short – Vida Groman; no middle name. The reader looked at my name, added up the numbers associated with each letter, turned to me and said, "You had a very difficult childhood."

I smiled and said, "How did you know?"

"Your name told me so," she said.

It was true. In order for my branches to grow, I needed healing so I could remember what the seed of me was meant to be. I started the healing – therapy sessions; talking and more talking. I became good at talking. One therapist said to me, "You could get a Ph.D. in insight." But still, I didn't change or feel connected to myself. I was missing something. By this time I was married, working for the State of Wisconsin, and looking so together to those around me. Only, my insides were almost constantly roiling and churning. I had married a very kind man and had a good job with great benefits for retirement, but it wasn't enough. I felt empty.

Years before, when I was twenty-one, I worked for a summer at a Fresh Air Fund camp in upstate New Jersey. Children from both the inner city and the countryside filled the row of cabins. I met the woman counselor who lived in the cabin next to mine. We would spend our downtime together, walking in the woods, talking about life. I remember her soft voice and caring energy. And I remember how I felt when I was with her. Have you ever walked into a place you have never been before and immediately felt at home? That is how I felt when I was with her.

Feeling at home was new to me. I always wanted to leave my childhood home and get away from my family. When people talked about wanting to go home for the holidays, I could feel their excitement about spending time with their families. My body would shudder thinking about going home to my family. But when I was with this person who happened to be a woman, I was at home in myself. I never told her how I felt. It was just a secret that I carried day after day during that summer. I felt like an adolescent at times. During my days off, when I went home to my family, I would suddenly feel like she was there. A flash of light or slight movement out the corner of my eye and my heart would begin to flutter with excitement that I might see her. I never considered that what I felt was love. But it was.

That summer ended. I didn't think about my attraction to women until my late twenties. I dated men, but never felt like I was at home. I just assumed something was wrong with me. Why wasn't I attracted to men? I went to therapy again, determined to fix it. In the meantime, I went to women's concerts, listened to Women's Music sung by Margie Adams, Holly Near, and Chris Williamson. Every time I sat in the theater amid gay women, I felt like myself.

I was a house divided though. My mind told me there was something wrong with me, yet the rest of me came alive when I was with other women who loved women. But in the late 70s into the 80s, it still wasn't okay to be gay. The thought that I might be gay was a foreign possibility. The only thing I knew to be true was that my feelings were authentic, deep, and so very life-affirming for me. But I ignored it and tried to deny it. I wanted to be a good family member, to be straight. Perhaps today, reading this, you might wonder what the big deal was. People today talk about their sexual orientation, gender identity, and more with ease, but it was not safe when I was walking into the experience of being fully myself.

The result of my denial was that I married.

We had an unusual wedding ceremony. Originally, we were to get married in the arboretum, a beautiful natural clearing the city had created for events like ours. Tall, majestic trees rose to the sky, surrounded by low ground cover that provided a natural cushion to walk upon. It seemed perfect.

The day of our wedding, we woke up early to get things ready. It began to pour, and it kept pouring. Rain kept coming down, wetting the ground and dampening our plans. The ceremony was quickly moved to our small house that we had moved into months before. Friends and family crowded around the wooden table in our small dining room. People scrunched up next to each other. Rabbi Swarsensky officiated. He was the only religious leader in Madison who would perform the wedding ceremony for interfaith couples, which we were. In just twenty minutes, we were man and wife.

The next morning, I woke up with the sickest feeling in my gut. I knew I had made a horrible mistake. I knew I was going to live a lie if I stayed in the marriage. Later, we revealed to each other that we knew it was the wrong decision, but felt we had to go through with the marriage anyway. Social pressure won out.

A year later, as part of my job working for the Bureau of Alcohol and Other Drug Abuse in Madison WI, I attended a five-day residential workshop facilitated by four women from Harrisburg, Pennsylvania. Thirty women from Wisconsin, Minnesota, Indiana, and Iowa came together to strengthen our leadership skills. During the last day, two of the facilitators taught us about "Minority Gut." We were being asked to grow our compassion for those different than us. Debbie, a Lebanese woman, spoke about how frightening it was to grow up in Johnstown, PA. Her story of isolation, ridicule, and hatred brought many of the women to tears. I remember hearing so many "Oh my Gods" from the group. Our hearts were softened by her pain. Our compassion grew.

Then Yvonne stood up. She spoke about her need to lie about her intimate relationship when she was with colleagues at the college where she taught. I listened to her words about the price she paid for that lying; she felt she was selling her soul to live with the secrets and denial of who she loved and was creating a life with. I listened from such a deep place, beyond what I was familiar with. I began sobbing where I sat in the corner of the room, quiet sobs, heart-wrenching sobs. I didn't feel like myself. Who was this person who was crying so hard her body shook? I looked around and nobody else seemed moved by Yvonne's story. Some women even expressed anger about this woman coming out.

"Why did she have to talk about this. After all, didn't she choose this?"

"If it is so uncomfortable, then unchoose it!"

I just kept crying.

One of the facilitators came over and gently approached me.

"I don't know what is going on, but something has just broken open in me," I confided.

She said, "I know. Don't try to figure it out right now. Just know when you go home to your husband, you may feel like your life has changed." I had no idea then how right she was.

The State of Wisconsin paid for my coming out!

I was twenty-nine years old when I came out. The trunk and branches of my tree were reaching out. My life was reaching out. This was the beginning of my journey of living life my way. All the old beliefs about relationships and being a responsible adult blew apart. I couldn't remain in the marriage relationship any longer, even though he was a kind man. There were so many sleepless nights as the internal battle of loyalty and betrayal played out, day after day.

If I follow what feels so true to me, won't
I hurt people I care about?

But don't I have the right to be me?

I grappled with those questions. There were so many times in my childhood when I gave in to the needs of others. So many times, to be loved and accepted, I said yes to them and no to myself. Something snapped in me and I knew I had to follow my own heart and be genuine.

Yes, there was hurt, plenty to go around. My husband said many times how he wished I had died. Hearing his words, I felt a stabbing in my heart. I felt like I should die, knowing my death would be easier for him to handle than being rejected because he was a man. I also felt his pain. I was stabbing him in the heart as well. He cried and asked who his emotional teacher would be now. I had to stand on my own two feet and tell him it couldn't be me anymore. I tried to let him know it was not about rejecting him as a man. No, it was about choosing me. The process of uncoupling felt like a breach birth. We were both being reborn, but it was a tough passage. For me, it was the first time in my life I had listened to my deep yearnings. Let me be honest, I was scared shitless!

I quit my job with the State and moved out of our house. I needed to drop the structure of my old life. I needed room to find myself. For the next six months, I lived on friends' couches while I waited for my next steps to begin. To pay for my lodging I washed dishes, cleaned houses, painted windows, refinished furniture, and finally worked as an assistant to an acupuncturist. I was free! There was time for long walks in the woods, time to listen to songs about women loving women, and time to read. I was on a pilgrimage back to myself, and as it turned out, back to my soul.

I learned to meditate and began reading stories of everyday people waking up to their spiritual nature. I was smitten. I was raised as a cultural Jew, which meant I identified as being Jewish but was not religious, so I never expected to experience what I did. One day as I was meditating, an image appeared in my mind's eye. Suddenly, I saw a silhouetted outline of a golden kingdom, with light shining so brightly off the surfaces of each building I squinted as I looked at the stunningly beautiful scene.

Then I heard the words, "The Keys to the Kingdom live within."

They were not just words. I could feel the truth- that I had all I needed within me. And what was within me was golden and more than I could ever imagine. Tears came into my eyes. My heart burst open. I had found my connection to the Invisible. That connection has guided most steps since then. I have come to believe that when I am connected with myself and with the Divine, my life flows in the direction that is right for me.

My sexuality and spirituality are inextricably connected. Before embracing my sexuality, I walked through the world in a very small, tight, scared container called *me*. When I said YES to who I was, I literally walked differently. I could feel my legs, my hips, and my body in ways I never had before. I felt alive! And in feeling that sense of being alive in my own body, I felt how expansive my energy was; the possibility that life was so much more than just what I saw come into being.

All those times, as a child, when I prayed there was more than the pain of my family, I didn't know that one day, I would step into my true self through my sexuality and that my sexuality would open me up to experiencing the Divine. I am grateful.

My Cousin Adolph

Adolph helped me love myself when I came out. A gay man, Adolph lived in New York City. He and Jake lived together for fifty years and married when they were in their nineties. Jake died first. Adolph died in 2018. A few years after Jake died, Adolph shared the story of their marriage. He said there was a long line of couples waiting to go into City Hall for the marriage ceremony. Adolph and Jake were the oldest couple in that line. When it was their turn, they walked inside, said yes to each other and walked out husband and husband. As they walked down the steps outside of the building, every couple waiting to do the same began clapping and cheering in celebration of the courage at their age to declare their love. I love that courage lives in my family.

Adolph was a talker. More importantly, he was a storyteller. When he and I would ride on a city bus in New York, he would point out different places of interest and tell stories about each one of them. He was so knowledgeable and interesting that within a few minutes, the rest of the people on the bus would turn around and listen to his stories. He widened my world. I visited for weekends when I was young and many times, his friends would visit. There was Marvin the accountant, Rose (Jake's cousin who taught opera), and Willie, an artist who lived in Greenwich Village. Willie always wore a big caftan that covered his large body. Jake would stand by the piano and sing opera while Rose played the piano. Willie drew a portrait of me when I was nine years old and I treasured it. A black line drawing, I kept it for many years before I unfortunately lost it. But the image still lives in my mind's eye.

When I came out in 1979, I called Adolph. I said I thought I was gay. He lovingly asked, "Are you sure?"

I said, "Definitely."

"Well then," he said, "you will be fine. At first," he continued, "your legs will feel shaky, like a chick coming out of its shell, but then you will live your life and be proud." I cherish those words to this day. His relationship with Jake was the most respectful relationship in my family. He and Jake were inseparable, and I loved spending time with both of those beautiful men.

Adolph gave me the gift of self-acceptance as a gay woman. And he gave me more than that, opening my eyes to other worlds, other ways of being. He planted seeds of curiosity and creativity in me, and I often find myself thanking him for being who he was.

I Want to Go Deep

I want to get deep with myself, to really connect with the depths of me. I want to have the courage to travel to my inner worlds, shine the light on the secrets of my soul. How can I explain that to anyone else? How can I find a way to walk through the world from these depths and stay connected with my inner wells while I still pay the bills, clean my house, and interact with others? I was told as a child that I was too much, too intense, too sensitive, all the while being treated as if I were not enough; too much, too little.

You already know how I loved to listen to music as a child. As I grew older, the music changed to folk music, songs about society, human emotion, human pain, and human joys. My eyes opened to the world and people not in my immediate experience. I grew a social conscience as I listened to Peter, Paul and Mary, Pete Seeger, and Ronnie Gilbert. They guided me with their words to know I was part of a village that included other people. I grew to know that what I did affected others. It was not about giving myself away, but about realizing there was me and there was the village I lived in. We affected each other. These singer-songwriters felt like deep friends who shared the desire to go deep. It was like we were from the same tribe; they let me hear the voice of my tribe.

Then came the music of women: Women's music. Holly Near, Tret Fure, Meg Christian, and many others – women singing the soul of women loving women to the world. They sang the ache of my heart, the secret in my heart, and I awakened to the truth of my loving, one woman with another; such stirrings in my heart, my hips, my breath. I remember being on a date with a man and we went to hear Margie Adams singing in a downstairs bar on State Street in Madison WI. I had never heard such soulful sound and expression of feelings before. I was entranced.

After the show I rushed up to her, for there were stirrings in me that I couldn't ignore. I had never been that bold. There she was, sitting at the piano talking with others equally excited about her music. I waited, my body stirring. Finally, she turned toward me and I asked, "Where can I buy your albums?" (no CDs at that time, of course). "Your music has touched me deeply; in a way I haven't felt before." I love that I had the courage to go up to her and speak, to give voice to my stirrings. She was singing my songs and I had the courage to ask. I apologize now to my date then – I forgot I was with him!

Here's the thing – when the truth of who we really are is revealed, the pull is irresistible. That pull, if we pay attention and follow it, will take us to heaven and back. And if we don't pay attention? Life has a way of getting our attention with ever-growing obstacles that finally get us to stop heading on the non-truth path. We get stuck and need to halt and examine our life for truth. Maybe it's through an illness, divorce, loss of a job, or depression. There are so many ways life can tug on our sleeves to get our attention. Music has always been a pleasurable, transforming way that life uses to get my attention.

Solitude

Many years ago, I read *Journal of a Solitude* by May Sarton (1992, WW Norton & Co, US). She wrote about her need for solitude:

> "I am here alone for the first time in weeks, to take up my 'real' life again at last. That is what is strange - that friends, even passionate love, are not my real life unless there is time alone in which to explore and to discover what is happening or has happened."

Every cell in my body vibrated with the truth of that quote. I really don't know what is true for me until I go off by myself, rid my mind of everyone else's voices and sit in quietude with myself. I don't know about you, but my everyday life is filled with sights and sounds of other people's opinions, ideas, and chatter.

Don't get me wrong, I love interacting, but if I don't take time for myself, I don't know what is happening in my inner landscape. If that goes on for too long, I become disconnected from myself and that leads to self-doubt, loneliness even while being with others, anxiety, and on and on it goes. I lose my ground. It is then I look outside myself, watching others and judging myself in comparison – and I always come up short. But when I choose (yes, I must choose) to break the pattern of disconnection, to be with myself, I can find my way back to wholeness and I remember that I am enough.

Here's the rub! Once my attention is so outwardly focused, I need to remember all of what I really want, how I really want to live, to pull me toward solitude. Several studies have shown that people would rather receive electric shocks than be alone, just themselves, with their own mind, body, and soul. This is tragic in my mind, to not know how to be with yourself in solitude. I am not saying it is always fun. It's not. And sometimes it is. That is not the point.

> *For me, it's about relationships – true,*
> *honest, authentic relationships. First with*
> *me, then with you. If I can't connect with*
> *me, how will I ever connect with you?*

I know it's not easy to turn inward. A woman in one of my workshops once said, "You are so nice and you made me feel so safe, but to tell you the truth, I'm just not into self-reflection." At first, I couldn't understand not being into the inner journey. I wondered how she spent her days. But I loved her honesty. She was kind. To me, she had her own connection with herself and that gave birth to that kindness. I realized her way was different from my way.

Sometimes, the process of going into solitude begins with me facing feelings that have been ignored for weeks, or even longer. Sadness, fear, and anger are the usual suspects. The hope is that by facing my feelings, I will remember my own heart and soul with tenderness. It's when I am willing to be honest with myself, to be in total truth, with tenderness, including uncomfortable and comfortable feelings, I grow my compassion for others.

Being with my own intense feelings allows me to sit with a woman who comes to work with me to share what she believes might scare the shit out of me. She musters up her courage to speak about what she feels is unspeakable, yet she has to speak it somewhere. And she's taking a chance with me. She is waiting for me to flinch. But I don't. I sit and breathe, and I am present, because I have done it with myself. I know what it's like to feel so negatively about my inside world of feelings that I assumed no one would stay with me, believing others would run away. So, I say to the women I work with, "Not much will send me running out the door. I have witnessed the range and depth of experience in my own life. I'm not a stranger to fear or pain."

So, I go back to May Sarton. I don't know who I really am or what I really want until I go into solitude with myself. It is my salvation.

One of those times of needing a solitude retreat took me to Richmond VA. There was a week-long retreat held in a building that was formerly a home for Catholic nuns. The building had been there since the Civil War. I put my belongings in my room, a small narrow space with one window at the end and a single bed against the wall, a small table beside it. I thought I could feel the essence of a nun's energy in that space. At lunch, I sat at a table with six other people. One person leaned over and asked why I was there. I took that question in deeply. I wanted to be able to answer with total honesty and authenticity. My answer was, "I came here to create a space to find my hunger. I want to know what I hunger for." I paused and breathed. He looked at me and said, "Write that down. It's a great title for a book."

Yes, creating spaces where we can find what we hunger for. Some call it our heart's desire. When I notice that I feel empty and disconnected from my deep well, the yearning bubbles up and lets me know what I hunger for. Truly, the hunger is always for my connection with me. Once that has occurred, I always open to the Divine, the

Sacred Connection with All That Is. And all fills in for me. The hunger ceases. Love abounds. Ideas float through and creativity emerges. The fear vanishes in the mist, rising to be absorbed by the ethers. Then I remember who I really am, a Spark of the Divine. I am at peace!

Facing Death in Peace

The phone rang. It was my sister, who was in Florida visiting my parents. As soon as I heard her voice, I knew something terrible had happened. My mother was sick – big-time sick. I was needed. I flew down as soon as I was able to get a flight to Del Ray Beach. That flight felt like a lifetime of moments. My childhood memories ran around in my mind's eye as I sat in the airplane seat counting the moments until I arrived in Florida. This was my mother, the parent I was closest to. I thought my heart would explode with fear. With each breath, I reminded myself to feel my feet on the floor of the plane. For now, I told myself, I was safe. I chose to believe my mother would be alright. The plane landed and I headed to my parents' home.

I took one look at Mom and saw illness in her face. Cheeks drawn; eyes yellow. My mom was having trouble breathing when she was up and moving around. She had been to the doctor, who wanted her in the hospital for further tests. What had started out as possible cardiac-related problems turned into the cancer diagnosis that quickly killed her. But for that moment, Mom was still there, scared and looking to her daughters to care for her.

She had surgery to remove the cancer the following day and was taken to the ICU for care. The nurses didn't tell us that sometimes people can experience ICU psychosis post-surgery. We were not prepared for Mom's reactions when we walked into her room. From her bed, she saw us walk in and began frantically calling us over to her side.

"What's wrong, Mom?"

"Don't tell them I am Jewish. They will kill me." If you remember, Mom and her family escaped from eastern Europe in her youth just before a Pogrom (military raid) on her village. She was terrified. She pulled me down toward her and begged that I go through her handbag and the garbage to remove anything that might identify her. I had never seen my mother so scared, ever. Michele and I were stymied. What should we do? Our decision was to play along with her fears to help soothe her. We picked through the small round metal wastebasket in the room, showing her we were getting the job done. Then we looked through her handbag and took out a few pieces of paper. And we promised her we would never tell anyone in that hospital that she was Jewish. She finally settled back onto her bed and sighed a sigh of relief. At last, she would be safe.

I couldn't believe what had happened during those ten minutes of terror my mother felt. She was seventy-four and had left her country when she was maybe four. So, seventy years had passed, yet still the fear lived in the cells of her body. I cried. My heart hurt so deeply for the leftover effects of actions taken against people almost seven decades earlier. Here was a woman about to face her death and she was being plagued by traumatic events from her childhood. I became very angry that she couldn't die more peacefully, and felt painfully aware of the long-term effects of hatred and violence. My mother has been gone thirty-five years now, and I still feel the intensity of that day whenever I think about it. My heart still breaks for the suffering we have visited upon each other through the ages.

Penny

A month before I went to Florida, I met the person who would become my partner for the next twenty-five years. Her name was Penny. She was my softball coach. A well-known fast pitch pitcher in the Midwest, who played in many softball tournaments, she decided not to play in the top women's league that summer. She wanted a break, so coaching a slow pitch team that was at the bottom of the league, which is what we were, seemed like a break for her.

I, on the other hand, was not an athlete. I really don't know what I was doing joining a slow pitch softball team. A friend had suggested I sign up. I had just ended a short-term relationship and was moping around. I guess my friend thought I needed a distraction. I said yes, but I was really thinking, "Why don't you just buy me season tickets to the theater?"

Seven years older than me, Penny had been in the gay women's community since she was twenty-three. She grew up in a family of Sicilian descent and was so very proud of her heritage. Every year, we attended the Italian Festa in Milwaukee WI to eat the luscious food and buy another Italian tee shirt. When we first met, she told me she wanted to live the rest of her life with me. I told her I needed to take it day by day, and then the years would add up to a life. We had our different ways of viewing the world.

There were ways in which Penny was very strong. She knew how to get things done on the physical plane. She knew how to gather people together and was good at putting her arms around someone in need and holding them. Emotionally, she was quite scared though. Early on in our relationship, Penny told me about the sexual abuse she had experienced as a young child. The man was a friend of her father, and the family didn't handle it very well. Mostly the abuse was excused, then ignored. Penny never really dealt with the abuse. Like so many, she hid it and didn't want to talk about it.

While Penny never attended college, she had an innate wisdom, and a highly attuned Shit Detector. She could read a person quickly to know if they had integrity or if they were full of shit. I was always amazed she could do that. I needed time and experience to know if someone was for real. I looked to her for "people readings." I remember when I first met someone I was considering working with and was pondering whether we would be a good match to teach together. Penny said she didn't trust that person. She just felt that energy. I didn't listen, and of course, Penny turned out to be correct.

Penny worked as the manager of her brother's Italian restaurant in Madison WI. She had a natural gift for taking care of people and easily created a welcoming environment there. However, while she was a gifted athlete and a natural caretaker, she felt "less than" others who had attended college. In other words, she often felt stupid. I never thought she was. She loved to learn by watching and reading. I'd ask her questions about different topics and she always seemed to know the answer, but that feeling of being "less than" never went away for her. The sexual abuse had left her with the belief that she was not enough, and that belief kept her from trying new things.

Penny needed to find another job when her brother sold the restaurant, but she was scared to apply. I took on two jobs to make sure we were financially okay. Over time, Penny's unresolved trauma took a toll on our relationship. She became more and more emotionally unavailable. It was painful for both of us. I had to make an excruciating decision. Although I loved Penny deeply, I couldn't continue to stay in a relationship where there was no flow of emotions and life. My soul was dying. We were no longer a couple.

We continued to live together for another year though. It was during that time I noticed Penny would ask the same question repeatedly, as if she didn't remember she had asked it a few moments before. There were other signs of a major shift in her cognitive processing. She would forget she was cooking something in the oven and then smoke would fill the apartment because the food had burned. I remember one time I found her in the kitchen, standing in front of the freezer, staring. Boxes of food were falling on her. I asked what was happening and she said she couldn't figure out how to get something she wanted out of there.

Penny was diagnosed with Vascular Dementia. She was in her late sixties. The hardest moments in the disease occurred in the early stages, when Penny would start crying and say, "Something is happening to me. What is happening to me? I am so scared." I would rush over to her, hold her in my arms and just breathe with her. It was all I could do.

That stage, when the person knows they are not who they have always been, is the cruelest stage. Once their awareness of self diminishes, that initial agony fades. At least, that is what happened with Penny. There were increasingly dangerous episodes where Penny would fall over at all hours of the night. Unable to take care of her by myself anymore, I had to ask her family to step in.

Eventually, Penny was moved into a nursing home for her remaining years. Dementia is a horrible disease that robs you of your loved ones. The person is there physically, but their awareness of you and the world around them slowly erodes and you fade from their view. As a friend put it, "It's a new reality each time you visit." Even though we were no longer together, I was devoted to Penny, and I visited her faithfully every Saturday for several years. She became childlike. Some people with dementia can become angry and violent; not Penny. She was sweet, funny, and very loving.

Before she moved into the nursing home, Penny lived with a caretaker. I was visiting her one day and the caretaker and I were having a conversation in another part of the apartment. The caretaker was telling me about her life and how she felt stupid at times because she didn't learn things easily. Even though Penny was watching TV, she overheard that part of the conversation and yelled from her chair, "Vida is not stupid." Then she returned to watching the movie she had watched twenty times before. She believed in me. I felt her loving me until she died.

I was blessed to see Penny a few days before she left her body. I asked a dear friend of mine to go with me to see her. This was because I wanted my friend to meet Penny in person, and because my friend was someone who knew so well how to be present with just about any human being with elegance and care. I sat near Penny's face. My friend sat at Penny's feet. I began to softly sing to her as I gently touched her forehead. My friend was holding her feet. Both of us were tenderly inviting Penny to relax and become open to her next steps.

Penny was no longer aware of this world. Her eyes were blank, her fingers were curled tight, and her body was frozen still. None of that was scary or uncomfortable for me. That time was sacred. For the past decade, I had been singing with The Threshold Singers of Madison, a service choir that sang at the bedsides of people who were dying. I am so very grateful to my choir for teaching me how to be present at this most precious time of life.

A few days after my visit, I received a phone call from Penny's niece to say Penny had passed. I felt such a mixture of emotions: deep sadness that I would never be able to see Penny again, but deep relief that she was free from then on. She had been ravaged by that disease for nearly a decade. It was time for her to move on. I cried deeply and called my friend to share the news. We talked about how beautiful Penny's energy was, how loving she was, and how I knew she loved me.

Penny and I were together for over twenty-five years and she was part of the fabric of my life. Memories of the good times came flooding in: the many Thanksgiving dinners, Passover dinners, gatherings at our home. I could see them clearly. Friends of ours often referred to Penny as a wonderful couch you could sink into, knowing she would hold you up. Before dementia took her down, Penny held me up in so many ways. I am deeply grateful.

An hour-and-a-half after I received the call, I taught a class to eleven women. I almost cancelled, but after talking with my friend, I knew I wanted to teach and dedicate the teaching to Penny. The program was called The Art of Feminine Presence®. I wanted to bring Penny's presence to the circle of women. I spoke from my heart, and they listened. We then talked about the power of the feminine. What a beautiful experience for me and what a wonderful way to honor Penny that was. I felt so guided to use the experiences of my life as a teaching to share with others. That way, everything has value.

My coming out both sexually and spiritually, my mother's death, and falling in love were the major events in my life that opened me up and shook me to my core. No longer could I act like I belonged in the mainstream of life. I had tried so hard though, working at a "regular job" at the state, marrying a kind man, and getting up every day and doing what everybody around me did. But that wasn't my way. I felt like I was being squeezed into a tight box and I was dying inside.

It took the loss of my mother and the reorientation to my way of loving to realize I needed to let go of the old to create the new. I just didn't yet know what the new was. A friend told me that choosing to walk on your true path takes courage and inner strength. She said this journey was not for the faint-hearted. It wasn't! My trunk had to be strong so my branches had the strength to reach out for what I truly wanted to be. I truly wanted to live from my heart and soul and teach others to do the same. The yearning to fully live burned in me so deeply. I was ready now to receive what was mine to teach.

PART FOUR

Flowers bloom, giving beauty to the world.
            Then the cycle completes.
        Seeds fall to earth to begin again.

Flowers to Seed Once Again

What is a flower but the culmination of the growing process of the tree? It is the reveal of what has gone on inside, from the soil to the seed opening, to the trunk growing tall and branches growing out. It is the gift given to the world. A lot goes into the growing of a flower: light, nourishment, the right conditions that foster growth, and so much more. Without all these supportive elements, a flower may never come to fruition.

For most of us, most of the time, we get enough support to produce some kind of flowering. Thank Goodness. And then what? What happens when everything does come together from the organic road map of creation? The world gets to benefit and flourish from the beauty the flower brings. The world benefits from our flowering, our gifts that have been given. We are uplifted by the giving as the world drinks in the juices of each of our offerings. And these offerings can be the simple expressions of our beingness. Every time we are who we truly are, I believe, the world benefits from the honest and authentic expression called Our Life.

As is told in one of my favorite movies, *It's a Wonderful Life*, one life affects so many others who go on to affect many more. To me, this message underscores the importance of each and every life on this planet. Each of us is part of the cosmic dance. No one is more important than anyone else. We all matter. So, we have a responsibility to take root and grow, with the help of others around us, so we can give of ourselves. We can give by simply and beautifully being who we are.

And in the end, when our flower drops to the ground to become seed once again, we can say to ourselves, "Well done. You did your best."

Where to Put My Left Foot

I was standing literally at the edge. This moment was the culmination of three days of emotional preparation for belaying down the side of a cliff. We had a choice of a 5-foot cliff or a 40-foot cliff. Our teacher, Dawna, said our learning would be the same, so it didn't matter which height we chose. Afraid of heights, I chose the 5-footer.

I remember the excitement I felt as I stepped into the harness, and how I had to make sure the harness was tight enough to hold me. There was a rope attached to the front of the harness and that was attached to a tree. You were supposed to lean back to test the rope, so I did. All this testing happened on flat ground near the edge. It reminded me of how excited I used to feel wearing my fencing outfit in college.

I fenced on the college team as the only lefty. I loved wearing the knee-length pants, white knee-high socks, white fencing shoes, the padded white jacket with the collar that covered my neck, and especially the metal mask that covered my face and head. Wearing the outfit was more fun than fencing. I only competed once and made the semi-finals. I gave a speech about fencing in front of my speech class and acted out the moves dressed in full array to applause. That earned me an "A" and a "Marvy" from the instructor. I probably should have majored in theater.

So there I was once again, in another "outfit," ready to go over the side of a cliff. I stepped backward slowly to position myself properly for the belay to begin. Tension mounted. If there were a drum nearby, that would have been the time for the drumroll to begin. I took a deep breath, leaned back… and let go.

I let go, only to end up with my feet in the air and my head toward the ground. I was hanging upside down, attached to my harness and rope, staring into the eyes of my other teacher, Andy, who was standing on the ground. He was there to help. I wasn't scared, only angry I had collapsed into that position.

"What would you like to do now, Vida?" Andy asked.

I said, "Don't do it for me. Just let me know where to put my left foot. I will do it for myself. I just need help to know my next step." Andy lovingly put his hand on a rock to my left and I placed my foot on it. That helped me get my bearings and I righted myself. It was a thrill to belay down the remaining few feet.

Even though it was only 5 feet, I learned so much about myself. Often, when I am about to take a big leap in life, at first, I collapse over the edge. My fear can turn me upside down for a while. It doesn't matter how much I plan. The magic occurs when I realize I am upside down and then I get curious about what might be my next step. It is in the getting up that I have grown my inner strength and belief in myself. And part of that getting up is opening to receiving guidance from within and from teachers around me.

Dawna Markova, My Teacher

I was born to be a ham. When I was young, I was shy. I was the one standing by my mother's leg for safety while I listened to her tell stories about her life. But somewhere deep inside me, the seed of silliness and theatrics grew. At summer camp I played Casey from the poem, *Casey at The Bat*. Dressed in a baseball outfit, holding a bat, I acted out the entire poem without ever uttering a word. My appetite was whet. Put me in front of a group and I would start running my shtick. Shtick is not telling jokes. No, shtick is observing what is going on around me and putting together a thought and observation that is funny. Yes, I was funny. I was serious also. But now we're talking funny. I would really light up whenever I was in front of a group.

In my forties, I began studying with one of my most important teachers, Dawna Markova. A group of eager students would meet five times a year for five days in a residential setting. Deep work, self-work, spirit work, work that took you to your knees. The peeling away of the detritus of the past. By the third night of each session, Saturday night, we needed some lightness and laughter to ease the process, so Saturday night became talent night.

Dawna saw something in me, something I didn't see, so she designated me as emcee. My job was to gather talent and facilitate the show. I loved it. I loved riffing in front of my community of beautiful souls who wanted to live more alive. Riffing for me is talking from my body. That is what I would do – look at the crowd, feel the energy out there, and then feel the energy in my own body. The words would come out of my body; sometimes serious, sometimes funny. People laughed, people were engaged, and I felt alive.

After several years of doing that, one weekend, Dawna challenged me to do what she called Stand Up. Stand Up was literally me standing up in front of a group of people and letting the stories and words come forward. She said when a person felt that ZAAAA (she loves sound), it was God giving you a sign that whatever brought on that ZAAAA was on your path. I took the challenge. I rented a local space and invited friends, who invited friends. My only requirement was that we all shared food before the show.

Over forty people showed up each of the two years that I did Stand Up. I was amazed and thrilled that people showed up – and some showed up twice! I have run workshops for years, teaching material I learned through Dawna and other teachers, but to stand on a stage and have people look at me, waiting for me to open my mouth, well, that is quite different, and frankly terrifying. It's like being naked in front of real people. They can see you! Thoughts such as "What will they think?" or "How will they feel about me when it is over?" go through your mind. That is the portal I walked through each time I stood on that stage, and still walk through every time I get up in front of a group.

It comes down to trust. I must trust myself and Spirit: trust Spirit that she will send me something, then trust myself to receive her. I used to feel that people would think I was shallow because I could do that thing of being funny. I wanted them to also see me as deep and serious with something of value to offer. I am a Sagittarian with a Scorpio moon. In fact, I have tons of Scorpio in my chart. I honestly don't know what all of that really means. I only know I can be very funny and very intense, and I must have both in my life to feel alive. I truly see that being in front of a group, teaching, is such a big avenue for sharing my gifts with the world.

To have someone see you, to see your gifts, and challenge you to use them in the world, is a blessing beyond measure. Dawna was that someone.

Moving Toward What You Want

I stood still, facing the wall on the opposite side of the room. Behind me, on the floor, sat my partner for the kinesthetic practice on breaking free from my past and going for what I want. Next to me on either side were other partners standing and sitting on the floor. I felt the two hands of my partner grasping my right ankle tightly. Very tightly. My job was to break free of the hold and head for my imagined "big want" on the other side of the room. It was up to me to choose my moment to go.

All I was thinking about was how my ankle hurt from the pressure of two hands holding it tight. I took a breath and tried moving forward, all the while focusing on those two hands holding me in place. By sheer force of will, I dragged my partner a few inches across the rug before I gave up.

"How is this like your life?" Dawna asked. "Oy! Do you have to ask?" I thought. "It has everything to do with my life!" I'd spent years telling the stories of my past repeatedly, and even though the telling became a mindless habit, the impact remained strong. Dragging my history with me led to constricted living.

Dawna invited each of us to claim the truth of our life. She asked us to recognize how our old stories held us captive. Thankfully, she told us there was a different way to move forward. We were invited to join our partners for our second attempt at moving to the other side, to what we wanted to create in our lives. As before, I stood facing the other side of the room and my partner, once again, took her two hands and grasped my ankle tightly. We had to start from that place of noticing what was holding us back.

I was learning that was just the starting point. That time we were invited to come into the present, into our presence. I felt myself drop into my body, legs standing strong. I breathed into my belly and felt the earth beneath me holding me up. Focusing on my belly rising and falling, I breathed the breath of life into my body. My attention was in the moment, not on what was behind me. I was ready to turn my attention to what I wanted, what I longed for.

I imagined that yearning waiting for me on the wall on the other side of the room and asked myself what I wanted. I answered, "I want to feel alive, to live vibrantly and exuberantly." I felt myself connect with that. It was what I had wanted since I was a child. Then I breathed. And, most importantly, I chose to move forward: all of me, forward.

What happened next was amazing. My ankle, held by two hands behind me, broke free of the hold! For a moment, I was so shocked by the freedom that I turned back to see shock on my partner's face as well, her hands in the air. I heard Dawna shouting, "Don't stop. Keep going. Don't stop till you get to what you want." In total exhilaration, all of me walked right across that room. When I reached the wall that held my yearning and desire, I took my hand and touched it. Standing there, touching what I yearned for, I breathed it into my body. Tears ran down my cheeks; tears of deep knowing that I could reach what I longed for.

I have never forgotten that kinesthetic metaphoric experience. It's one thing for someone to tell me I can have what I want, but it's another thing for me to feel that in my body, in my bones. To know how to come to the present moment in such a way that allows me to acknowledge my past while claiming the now is one of the most profound learnings in my life.

Let me be clear – this isn't a one-time practice. This isn't a parlor game. No, this is a life practice of being willing to notice when I am being held captive by my past, to name it, and then choose to bring myself back to this present moment. And from this present moment, to ask myself what it is that I need, what it is that I want, and what it is that serves my highest good. I can then uncover my next steps, much like Andy showed me on that cliffside when I was upside down. I've come to believe and know that this is how to create my path. As Joseph Campbell said (goodreads.com//quotes/21396-if-you-can-see-your-path-laid-out-in-front):

> "If you can see your path laid out in front of you step-by-step, you know it's not your path. Your own path you make with every step you take. That's why it's your path."

I have learned that my path comes from inside me. As a kid, I used to try to see my future. I would literally strain my eyes trying to see years ahead. I couldn't. The only result of my efforts was headaches. I didn't know then that I needed to go *in* before I go out. I didn't know I needed to go to the depths of myself, my heart and soul, to ask what was true for me.

What I did learn early on was to look outside of myself, to see what and how others were doing things. I did that long enough that my connection to myself became a faint whisper, difficult to hear. And yet, I knew I needed that connection to wake up.

My real life wasn't about what others did or thought about life. I just didn't know how to make that inward journey, how to wake up the sleeping light within me. Dawna Markova taught me how and I am forever grateful to her.

Alice Tredway, My Guide

Alice lived in the city of Munising, which is in the Upper Peninsula of Michigan on Lake Superior. The city was co-founded by Alice's husband. Forty-two years younger than Owen, Alice was the second Mrs. Tredway. The first died of cancer and Alice was her caretaker. Mr. Tredway and Alice developed a tender relationship during his first wife's illness. When he proposed to Alice, Alice's mother told her she would only allow the marriage if Alice kept friends her own age. They married and had two daughters.

By the time I began working with Alice, Owen had died, and her daughters were full-grown women with children of their own. Alice tells the story of Owen's death that opened the door for her special and unique past life work, which became nationally known.

"Owen went into the hospital due to an illness. In the middle of the night, I sat bolt upright and said, 'I want to know what Jesus knew about healing.'" She looked at the clock. Shortly after that moment, the hospital called to say Owen had died. The time was the same as when Alice finished making her demand of Spirit.

After Owen died, Alice began her work. She took people into their past lives to heal the present. When you worked with her, you had to go to her house, and for $150, you lived with Alice for six days, cooked meals together, drove to Marquette, Michigan, to buy fish cheeks, and took her to a supper club once for dinner. The rest of the time was spent from morning till late evening doing the work. With the help of her guides, Jesus, Lao Tzu, Edgar Cayce, St. Peter, St. Mary and more, she guided you into the past lives you needed to explore for your layer of healing at the time.

My first meeting with Alice happened during the winter of 1980. My first partner was scheduled for her six-day experience. Several weeks prior to that, we decided to drive to Munising for a skiing trip. Susan and I arrived at midday and called Alice. She invited us to what I call a Salon that was being held at her home. We walked into a room crowded with women of different ages. Some sat on couches, some on the floor. I found a space by Alice's feet and quietly sat down.

There I was, sitting at the feet of a woman in her seventies, long gray hair pulled back in a ponytail, wearing a brown velour top and pants. She sat relaxed and attentive in her chair, with her legs tucked underneath her. Women asked questions about life then and life from their past. As I listened and watched, I felt so connected to Alice. I couldn't understand why; after all, this was so new to me. When there was a pause in the conversation, I mustered up my courage and shared that I felt so close to her and didn't know why.

She turned to me, softly looking into my eyes and told me, "You were probably at the Cross at the time of Jesus' death."

My mouth hung open. "What?" I said to myself, "how could that be?" After all, I was a Jewish girl from New Jersey in this lifetime and didn't know much about Jesus. Alice said that people who worked with her knew Jesus. Then the group conversation simply continued. My mouth still hung open. I didn't know what to make of what I'd just heard, but there was something about Alice. I knew I had to work with her.

And I did, for the next five years, until her death at seventy-eight years old. Every year, I drove the eight hours north from Madison Wisconsin to Munising, Michigan to spend six days with Alice. It was during those sessions I learned about my past lives, the people I knew in the present who were in those previous lives, and what lessons I still had to learn. In my first session with Alice, I learned that the purpose of my current life is to love God. Oh, how I have danced with, resisted, and surrendered to that purpose through the years. Alice opened me up to my connection to Spirit and the Invisible worlds. In the teachings of the Kabbalah, a form of Jewish mysticism, it is said that what we see around us is only 5% of reality – 95% is invisible. Alice took me to the invisible. I remembered who I had been and who I wanted to be going forward.

After four years of working together, Alice told me she would not charge me any money for the work because she and I were colleagues. We would work on each other. I had been doing my own energy work with people by this time. The six-day visit that year was the most sacred time I had ever spent with her. We worked all day long, as usual, but this time, she told me stories of her lives. She let me see into her. She was vulnerable and tender with me. I felt so blessed to be able to share my gifts with her and feel her receiving what she needed.

One particularly humorous evening happened at the supper club. Everyone knew Alice, her history with Owen and her work. She was often referred to as, "Crazy Mrs. Tredway." Alice was losing her hearing by then, so you had to talk quite loudly for her to hear you. Alice began talking about Nostradamus and told me he had called her the previous week. I yelled back, "Who is Nostradamus?"

"That guy from Colorado I told you about," she yelled back. People turned around to look and I just smiled. I loved Alice and all her beautiful layers and colors of her soul, even though she wore that same brown velour outfit much of the time.

Mary Ebert, My Writing Angel

Alice Tredway introduced me to Mary Ebert, a therapist from central Wisconsin. Later in life, she became the writer of blessings for folks who somehow found her. And so, I had found her. I requested a few blessings through the years. Mary used to say she would wait for her cat, Charlie, to rub against the legs of the table on which her typewriter lived. Then she knew it was time to receive someone's blessing. If you asked her when to expect your blessing, she would say, "It's up to Charlie."

Within a few years of my meeting Mary, she was diagnosed with Parkinson's disease. She then required a caretaker to help her with her daily needs. One time, her caretaker had to go home so Mary was without help. My partner, Penny, and I said we'd be happy to have Mary stay with us. Penny was a most loving caretaker with Mary. I got to watch love meet love with those two women. Each knew how to stay in the moment and be in their heart. That is love meeting love to me. Watching them was powerful. I had spent most of my life trying to run away from illness, physical or mental, so watching Penny be present with Mary and watching Mary receiving from Penny opened my heart.

During Mary's stay with us, I revealed that I wrote poems, or as I called them, Writings from Spirit. She asked to read them. It took a lot of courage for me to bring those stories, those writings, out of their hidden places into the light. I watched Mary read them as I sat in my own vulnerability. Then she said, "Vida, please keep writing. Spirit wants you to write." I thanked her for those words of encouragement, of belief in me. I had kept my writings in the dark for many years. Mary gave me the permission to shine the light on my words that came from Spirit. Remembering Mary's words has kept me writing, an invitation for me to open to Spirit through all these years. I am eternally grateful.

I wrote a poem to celebrate Mary and fortunately, she got to read it before she died.

For M.E. From V.G.

> There was once
> And always a woman,
> A wonder-filled
> Woman who gave
> Blessings.
> Blessings that reverberated
> Throughout the
> World – rippling outward,
> Touching one, touching many.
>
> Now the time came
> For the rippling
> to come home because she,
> The wonder-filled woman,
> Needed the ripple.
> So, she became the Receiver of Blessings,
> Even just for one small moment.
>
> And we, who had received so much,
> Watched the Giver of Blessings
> Receiving, and we smiled.

Those two women, Alice Tredway and Mary Ebert, opened worlds for me, opened me to me. They believed in me. They saw me in my own Vidaness. I think about what it was like early in my life when I stood out like a sore appendage because I was different from the girls I grew up with, not knowing why I didn't fit in, not knowing I was to take a road that was so different from my family and community. I was lonely, uncertain at the beginning. But those two women gave me space to be me. It has truly been the *Long and Winding Road* back to me.

When I was a guidance counselor, I loved working with those kids you would describe as living off the beaten path, off the path of familiar scenery. Even now, the women who come to me walk paths that are unique. They create their steps one foot in front of the other, wanting so much to find their home, not to fix, but to repair, to connect with themselves once again. I love these women for wanting to find their way home.

Sacred Sovereignty

I heard these two words many years ago. They came through Spirit. I was told I was to help women stand in their own sovereignty, their own power. When they did that, that was sacred, holy, elegant, and of high quality. That is what I hold on to when I connect with the woman who wants my support. I want to guide that soul back to herself to claim, name, and aim her essence in the world.

In the Jewish tradition, there is something called Tikkun Olam – repairing the hurt in the world. When a woman stands in her sacred sovereignty, I believe she is helping to mend the tear in the fabric of the planet. When she stands tall, believes in herself, loves herself, even just a bit, when she knows how to speak up and out, is fierce in her compassion and integrity, she is a catalyst for change, for rebirthing and loving. We become fierce, loving mothers to our families, communities, and the world.

Feminine energy and presence are powerful. I believe we are here to be the breath in to the breath out, to the breath in. It is the time for women to stand, speak, show, and be seen.

This poem came to me as I pondered the generations of women in my life and how important it is to me to remember I am here because of those women who went before.

Generations of Women

The Grandmothers who have come before us.
We, the women of the present, stand on their
shoulders as we walk forward.
I hope we can embrace our past women and not
turn our back on them.

On the Shoulders of Our Grandmothers

We look forward, taking steps, one foot after the
other.
What is the ground on which we walk?
It is the ground of the Grandmothers,
the women who walked before.
These women who struggled to find their place
by choice, not by role.
These women who risked it all so we can say we
belong, we have wisdom, we have bodies that feel
and bleed and give birth.
We will not be quiet.
We matter.
This is the ground on which we walk.

Don't forget them. Don't turn a deaf ear to them
because they're old or no longer here in body.
Use their wisdom.
Learn from their mistakes and celebrate their
triumphs.

As you, the new women, walk into the uncharted
lands filled with new and old landmines,
Know that you are held by these Grandmothers.

And to the Grandmothers, now alive and gone
from body,
Open to seeing your granddaughters in their
strength and vibrancy.
You gave birth to them.
Give them room to move about, fly, fall down, get
up and create newness.
Bless them, trust them, love them.

Let us all come together as in a golden
shimmering cloth, a tapestry if you will.
Then in that coming together, the fabric becomes
even stronger.
This is the time for women of heart, of soul,
of openness, fierceness of commitment, and
tenderness of action.

In my thirties, I remember standing in the doorway to Tonta Frumi's
bedroom. I was watching my great aunt standing on a stool while my
aunt was hemming her dress. My mother was lying on the bed and
my sister and her daughter were sitting on a chair. They were talking
and laughing, engaged in the stuff of women. Generations getting
older and new generations coming up. I saw the history of women
as I listened. I was a part of that flow, generation to generation. I was
part of the lineage of women of my family. I imagined ancestor after
ancestor in that moment.

It was a moment without words. I was standing on the shoulders of my grandmothers. Only now, I am considered to be an older one, a grandmother, even though I have no physical grandchildren. I am becoming the ground on which new women, younger women, are walking. And on and on it goes. Blessed are the women: young, old, gone, and yet to be born.

PART FIVE

In the end, we are not just one moment.
  A tree doesn't have just one leaf.

        We are a wonderful array
          of every moment of our living.

This Moment is Made Up of Millions of Moments

I stand back as if on the edge of a cliff, looking out over the horizon around me, seeing the expanse, feeling the breeze of the air, temperature just right, my skin alive. I ask, "Who am I? Who am I here, right now?" My answer is whoever I am, I am made up of millions of moments of living, of loving, of crying, of raging, of feeling joy. I am all of these and more, beyond my five senses. I am Jack and Ruth's daughter, their younger daughter. They gave birth to me. They also gave me insight, sensitivity, and a sense of being grounded, not directly, but by way of the grueling pain they both lived with. I looked at them both, my parents, Ruth and Jack, and said, "There must be more than this to living. There must be light and love and heart. Please let there be more." And there was.

All that I have lived is in my veins, my blood. All that I am now is there as well. I chose to take what has come my way and make something of it. My mother's saying, "Something doesn't come from nothing," holds even more true now. I also know I am not finished. I stand on the ground I am on now, today, hoping I have years ahead of me to continue learning, sharing, and meeting new people who will teach me about living from my heart and soul.

When I am About to Die

When I am about to die, if someone asks me about my life, if I lived it well, what would I say? I would say I lived it as best as I could, always open to the next piece to grow into. I would say I lived it with presence, with joy and heart, that I was honest, and touched as many lives as I could with love and compassion. I would say I contributed what I knew, that I laughed, and I stayed flexible of mind and heart, and I learned to love – myself and others. That feels true and right. I could rest easy then.

What I Have Learned

Spirit once told me, "The hardest thing you will ever do is to face the parts of yourself you hate. The most healing thing you will ever do is to face the parts of yourself that you hate." I have practiced the turning toward me all my life and I have learned that life is about loving and compassion. These are words to grow into over and over again.

Imagine accepting yourself as you are,
without the fixing.

Spirit said I was to help people RE-PAIR. I was sitting on the front steps of my house and that was what I suddenly heard. I was livid and began arguing with Spirit. "What do you mean help people repair? They are not broken. They are not TVs to be fixed." Spirit held me close and got my attention. And then I heard, "Look at the word, Vida! RE means again. Pair means come together. So dear one, you are to help people to repair, to come together with themselves again."

Ah, I breathed. Yes, I can say yes to that. So here I am, now as I was then, teaching myself how to repair with me. Teaching myself how to love me, how to fall in love with me, with all my thorny, bitchy, tender, funny, wise, loving parts – a patchwork blanket of humanity. At seventy-three years old, I have been telling folks that I'm finally falling in love with myself.

PART SIX

What have we harvested?
What have we gained by our living...

Ah, to rest and reflect as we sip a cup of tea.

The Harvest – The Gift
This Book has Given Me

No one can accuse me of living an unexamined life. When I was in my late teens, someone told me they thought I thought too much about everything, to a fault. I went home and spent the rest of the day thinking about what they said about me. So now, of course, I am thinking about this process called "writing a book." I am asking myself why I would even think about writing about my life for others to see and perhaps judge, and I am asking how the writing of this book has changed me, for I know it has.

I have been moved by the life stories of others, helping me see and feel lives I might never have imagined. I get larger, more expanded, by opening to new ways of living. And when those stories show me how to move through the pain of being human, I receive the playbook for my own life. If that person could rise above their challenging childhood and claim their gifts and talents to share with the world, then so can I.

And now it is my turn to share my stories for others to read and hopefully learn from. Back in my forties, I knew I wanted to write a book, but felt I hadn't lived long enough yet to have stories worth sharing. I have lived long enough now; I know that. The book that has been living in me has risen to the surface to show itself. So, I wrote it.

It is a funny thing, this writing about your life. For almost a year, I couldn't stay still long enough to sit down and look at a blank screen on my computer and find words to begin. I found every excuse I could to do other things. My apartment was very clean because I could always find something to vacuum, dust, or wash. I knew it was time to put words to "paper," but a part of me kept me from beginning. What was I afraid of? I was afraid of something, clearly.

Early on in my healing journey, I remember being in a therapy session and the counselor remarked to me that I was so gifted at noticing others' pain but seemed to be oblivious to my own. I was taken aback by her observation. What was she talking about? Later that night, I had a dream. I was in a kind of art gallery. On the walls were portraits of every member of my family, painted in great detail, showing their pain. But nowhere did I find my own portrait. Where was I? I was willing to see their pain, but not mine. It was as if I were "blind" to me. This book that wanted to be written was asking me to "SEE" me. I was being asked to turn toward myself and take a good look at me. And in that turning toward me, I was being asked to see that I made it. Not only did I survive, but I also thrived, and am still thriving.

With every memory or reflection that came through me, I had to breathe, and remember. In the remembering, I re-membered my life. I connected with once forgotten or ignored moments of my experience that contributed to me being me. I saw my vulnerabilities and found myself feeling so tender toward each one. I could see and reclaim my foibles, my failings, as well as my moments of courage and growing strength. And, as if I were looking at my portrait in the gallery of my life for the first time, I knew I was seeing and falling in love with me. The book was having its way with me!

I am forever changed. There is nothing like seeing what has been hidden, feeling what was not felt, and hearing words that needed to be said and written down. A wholeness. A courageous act of reclamation. I have studied and experienced many tools for healing in my life and

I bow to them, for I gained strength and skills to walk through my life and create offerings in the world. But writing a book about my life has given me a new sense of myself. I feel my whole body these days. And through that body awareness, I experience more belief in myself.

I know I exist. I know I have grown from a seed in the soil to a trunk with branches reaching out. I know I have produced flowers to give to others. I know because I can see it –right in front of me, on paper.

I finally can see me.

This book, my teacher, has revealed to me several important lessons that I want to pass on to you.

The Importance of Remembering Your Life

The first is the importance of remembering your life. As I said earlier, our past is the foundation upon which we stand. Painful or not, our past experiences color how we respond to current situations in our life. To not be aware of our past is like trying to walk forward with a rope tied around our ankle. It is difficult to move anywhere because that rope is tied to what is behind us. We keep trying, but we get pulled back and wonder why we repeat patterns over and over again. When we choose to remember our lives, when we say yes to turning toward where we came from, we can open doors to our light that we have been hiding, consciously or unconsciously. It's what makes me "me" and makes you "you."

I invite you to find your way to turn toward where you have come from. Step into the soil you grew up in, not to wallow in it but to learn from it. It won't be easy, but it is truly worth it. You will gain yourself. If you don't turn toward your life, you will just keep repeating the past and live a life half-lived.

Honor Who You Really Are

Once you do that, the book revealed to me, it is time to honor who you really are. It is so important to uncover what has been living there all along – your unique light, and how it wants to shine in the world. For me, that light needed to know it doesn't matter who is the object of my love – what does matter is that I follow my heart.

My heart led me, and continues to lead me to my next steps. I don't follow a path that is well-worn. I know now that if you can see the path in front of you, it is not your path. Your path is created with each step you take. How do I know what that next step is? I must be connected to my heart. I must learn how to live in my body, not my head. If I hadn't found the courage to love who I was meant to love (for me, that is another woman) I would not have been able to open to life.

Trying to fit in is not the answer, ever. So, I invite you to find the support you need to learn how to connect with your body, heart, and soul so you can walk each step of your unique path in life.

Recognize We Don't Ever Live This Life Alone

Lastly, the book reminded me that I don't ever live this life alone. There have been so many mentors, teachers, and friends of many kinds who have held me and guided me in my journey. I continue to meet wonderful, powerful people who through their own courage and vulnerability show me how to live more truly alive. I would not be here without them.

Sometimes these people have first appeared as "enemies" or "challenges." In time, they have turned into my "Sacred Enemies" who have taught me how, and how not, to live. Sometimes, I have just a few moments with a person, and I leave with a life-altering lesson. Some people have walked with me for decades. The mind can convince us we are alone, and that is one of the most horrible lies we can believe, for it leaves us deeply lonely and frozen.

I will never forget the elderly woman I spoke with for just a few moments one day at the grocery store. She was pushing her cart down the aisle, coming toward me. We both stopped and began talking. On the surface, it sounded like nothing, but there was an energy of love and connection. At the end of the brief encounter, she asked if I went shopping there at the same time every week, because she did, and wouldn't it be wonderful if we met again. Her kind heart, her open heart, touched me deeply – connection.

Unfortunately, I never saw her again, but I still remember her kindness to me. As I moved to another aisle, a young woman stopped me and told me she had walked by the two of us in the other aisle. She wanted me to know how deeply moved she was by our kind interaction, by the energy beneath the words. One interaction led to three people being deeply touched.

We do affect each other. We need each other, and we are all teachers and mentors to each other. Look around you. Let yourself see, feel, and hear who is beside you. Who was beside you in the past? Who have you stood beside?

Remember

Remember…
The day you first opened your eyes, and in that
opening you gained the world.

Remember…
The moment your heart first broke open to love
more deeply, how you hurt and thought you'd
never make it through when it ended, but you
did, and you learned what love is and isn't for
you.

Remember…
How it felt when snowflakes landed on your
face, the cold wet wonder of that unique form
of Godness, and then the flakes melted because
the warmth of your alive body met their small
coldness.

Remember…
Your love of little moments of laughter with
friends, knowing you belonged, and still
belong, to a circle of those who get you, see you,
understand you, and still love you.

And mostly, remember to remember big
moments, and micro moments of your life, for
they go by quickly and die if we don't remember
to take the time to remember.

Thank You

Thank you for taking time to journey with me. My hope is that you have found some tender moments with yourself and your life as you read these stories and reflections.

I would love to share a blessing I wrote for myself with you. I hope this may inspire you to write one for yourself.

Blessing for Herself

To be free,
Alone, together.
To walk wide on a
Five-lane path.
To share that path
With another, with lots of others.
To hold a hand,
Tenderly, loosely,
Yet with deep feeling
And commitment.

To feel the breeze
In my hair,
To see the mountains wide
Surrounding my being,
To walk with an open heart.
All this and more do I wish for myself.

Gratitude

I give thanks to the following people, without whom my journey would never have come this far. Each of you, in your own way, has been witness, coach, supporter, and believer in me. Thank you for the hours, days, months, and years of supporting me being me. You are the best!

Dawna Markova and Andy Bryner, my origin teachers. Without you, I am not sure I would have begun my journey of finding my own way of being. You taught me to come home to myself, to trust myself.

Julie Ann Turner, I thank you for bearing witness to my journey at a time when I didn't know if I could travel any further because all I thought was holding me up had been stripped away. Your guidance and deep caring kept me on track. Thank you, Sistar.

Rachael Jayne Groover, you came along when I needed a community of like-souled and like-hearted women. I knew when I first watched you talk about the importance of being in one's body that you spoke my language and you would understand what I needed to grow beyond my believed limits. And in your capacity to create a committed community, I have found a home. You lovingly challenge me to stretch beyond and beyond.

Datta Groover, thank you for allowing me to find safety with you, a strong and tender-hearted man. You have supported me in finding my voice, and for that I am eternally grateful. Thank you for helping me give birth to this book. Thank you for understanding how I write and for giving me the phrase, "poetic prose."

Richard Slade, thank you for the many hours of guiding me back to me. Your belief in me, your loving heart, have always reminded me that I am worth it and that all the answers lie within.

Sisters of the Pen, Lucy, Teresa, Paula, Gina-Dianne, and Lisa, I look forward to each week when we take pen in hand, inspire each other to write and then share those precious words with each other. It takes a village. You five are a real part of my village. Deep gratitude!

Jody Whelden, evolutionary sister and friend, thank you for being there through the ups and downs as we both took, and still take, our next steps in our evolutionary journey toward wholeness.

Annie Powell, soul sister and friend, how many hours have we talked about life, creativity, love, and good movies? Never enough! Thank you for letting me reveal my soul.

Amara Hamilton, thank you for getting me. Thank you for guiding me with my energy and for being such a grounded energy for me. I see and feel your tender and strong heart.

And thanks to my family and many wonderful friends who are part of my village!

About The Author

Healer, teacher, speaker, writer, and facilitator of transformational experiences for women, Vida Groman has walked the evolving path of spiritual growth and championed "finding your own way of being" all her life.

In over thirty-five years of service to women, Vida has gently and clearly guided women to stand in their Power and Passion as they create the lives they desire and deserve, from a center of Sacred Sovereignty.

Vida's popular *LifeSwitch*™ series inspires audiences worldwide. She also loves facilitating circles and groups, and bringing her writing and message alive through her voice. Vida was selected and showcased as one of thirteen writers for the national *Listen to Your Mother* show, where she read her original piece *My Mother's Name is Ruthie,* honoring her mother.

Today, Vida speaks, teaches, coaches, and continues to write and publish her poetic prose. Find her work at **vidagroman.com**

Vida has an MS in Counseling, is a Certified Soul Directed Healer, Personal Thinking Patterns Consultant, Certified Professional Coach, Certified HeartMath Teacher, and Licensed Art of Feminine Presence® Teacher.

The Artwork

Thank you, Christine Banman, for your wonderful and alive images in my book.

Christine's own words:

> I have been painting and creating my entire life. My mom is my original teacher. In 2011, I realized I could paint and create, and people wanted me to spread some beauty to the environment around us. So, I did, and I have been going strong ever since. My main intention with my art is to stir emotion. Even if you walk by a painting of mine and stop, and your lips curl just a little bit, I feel my job is complete.

Made in United States
North Haven, CT
15 September 2024

57474114R00100